100

❧ Days *of* ❧

FAVOR

Joseph Prince

CHARISMA
HOUSE

Most CHARISMA HOUSE BOOK GROUP products are available at special quantity discounts for bulk purchase for sales promotions, premiums, fund-raising, and educational needs. For details, write Charisma House Book Group, 600 Rinehart Road, Lake Mary, Florida 32746, or telephone (407) 333-0600.

100 DAYS OF FAVOR by Joseph Prince
Published by Charisma House
Charisma Media/Charisma House Book Group
600 Rinehart Road, Lake Mary, Florida 32746
www.charismahouse.com

Unless otherwise noted, all Scripture quotations are taken from the New King James Version®. Copyright © 1982 by Thomas Nelson. Used by permission. All rights reserved.

Scripture quotations marked AMPC are from the Amplified Bible, Classic Edition. Copyright © 1954, 1958, 1962, 1964, 1965, 1987 by The Lockman Foundation. Used by permission. www.Lockman.org

Scripture quotations marked KJV are from the King James Version of the Bible.

Scripture quotations marked NASB are from the New American Standard Bible, copyright © 1960, 1962, 1963, 1968, 1971, 1972, 1973, 1975, 1977, 1995 by The Lockman Foundation. Used by permission. www.Lockman.org

Scripture quotations marked NIV are from the Holy Bible, New International Version. Copyright © 1973, 1978, 1984, International Bible Society. Used by permission.

Scripture quotations marked NLT are from the Holy Bible, New Living Translation, copyright © 1996, 2004. Used by permission of Tyndale House Publishers, Inc., Wheaton, IL 60189. All rights reserved.

Scripture quotations marked TLB are from The Living Bible. Copyright © 1971. Used by permission of Tyndale House Publishers, Inc., Wheaton, IL 60189. All rights reserved.

This publication is translated in Spanish under the title *100 días de favor*, copyright © 2011 by Joseph Prince, published by Casa Creación. All rights reserved.

Visit the author's website at www.josephprince.com.

Library of Congress Cataloging in Publication Data:
Prince, Joseph, 1963-
  100 days of favor / Joseph Prince.
    p. cm.
  Includes bibliographical references.
  ISBN 978-1-61638-449-4
  1. Meditations. 2. Bible--Meditations. I. Title.
  BV4832.3.P75 2011
  242'.2--dc22
                                        2011012331

Published in association with: Joseph Prince Teaching Resources
www.josephprince.com

20 21 22 23 24 — 20 19 18 17 16
Printed in the United States of America

Introduction

I'VE GOT A challenge for you that I believe will change your life! I want to challenge you to take a journey with me for the next 100 days. Let's plunge headfirst into the vast ocean of the Lord's unmerited favor. In the world that we live in today, it's so easy to forget the Lord's unconditional love for each of us. It's so easy to forget that the Lord Himself is personally interested in making you a success in every area of your life.

If you would simply set aside these 100 days to just immerse and saturate yourself in the unmerited favor of God, I believe with all my heart that your life will never be the same again. Every morning as you are sitting with a warm mug of coffee in your hand, simply pick up this book. I'd like us to spend 15 minutes together and have an intimate chat about Jesus. I believe that these precious minutes will help you calibrate your thinking for the rest of the day. And when your mind is set on the favor of the Lord, you will begin to experience like never before a confident expectation of good, regardless of the adversity or challenge that is thrown your way.

My friend, when you begin living with the consciousness of God's unmerited favor, you will savor and enjoy the beautiful plan and purposes that God is unfolding in your life. When you focus on His grace, His favor and His love for you daily, you are putting a magnifying glass over your life and allowing Jesus' love to beam down upon you in all its radiance, beauty and warmth. No matter what may be happening around you, you will be anchored in the security of His perfect love, hidden in the cleft of the immovable Rock of all ages—your loving Savior, Jesus Christ.

This is an invitation to take the next 100 days as a commitment to soak yourself in the unmerited favor of God. Pull yourself away from the noise, chaos, clutter and busyness of life, and come under the refreshing waterfall of God's favor. Take this time to simply sit at Jesus' feet and enjoy His Word. You'll find the stress of work, family commitments, people's expectations and even the fear of the future melting away.

100 Days Of Favor is based on my book, *Unmerited Favor*. Each bite-sized, inspirational reading includes:

- *Today's Scripture*—A scripture that relates to the inspirational reading, giving it a biblical foundation and helping you to understand the truths presented. I encourage you to meditate on each scripture for the day. You'll be surprised how much the Holy Spirit will open up God's Word to you and refresh your heart!

- *Today's Inspirational Excerpt From* Unmerited Favor—A key truth or nugget about God's unmerited favor that will surely equip, bless and empower you. These truths cover what God's unmerited favor is, what it can do for you and how you can develop favor-consciousness to experience good success.

- *Today's Prayer*—Don't know what or how to pray for a breakthrough? These prayers will help you express all that's in your heart to your heavenly Father. Feel free to adapt them to your own situation. Just speak from your heart. The effective, fervent prayer of a child of God avails much. Your Father is listening!

- *Today's Thought*—The mind is where the real battle usually takes place. So start your day with a liberating, favor-inspired thought. The best way to guard your mind is to fill it with God's precious thoughts toward you!

- *Today's Reflection On Favor*—As you prayerfully read each day's inspirational word, take time to journal the things that the Holy Spirit brings to your attention and encourages you to meditate on.

Make your personal journey into the depths of God's unmerited favor a powerful and purposeful one!

It's so important for you to develop a favor-consciousness in everything that you do because our human tendency is to depend on our own strengths to succeed. It's so easy to revert to self-effort—where we end up striving and worrying—instead of depending on God's favor for success in all areas of our lives. So let's take these 100 days to completely saturate and lose ourselves in the vast beauty of His unmerited favor!

Grace always,

Joseph Prince

A Special Note From The Author

Understanding Biblical Meditation

MY FRIEND, AN exciting adventure awaits you! But before you embark on day one of your journey into discovering God's unmerited favor, there's something burning in my heart that I just have to share with you. In fact, I asked my publisher to hold back the printing of this book just so that I could add this special note to you, one that I firmly believe will help make your journey fruitful and life-transforming.

The Lord had been speaking to me in my quiet time about the importance of meditating on His Word. Then, something extraordinary happened during a recent trip to Israel. I was there with some of my church's key pastors and leaders, whom I affectionately refer to as my "band of brothers." As we were trekking down Mount Arbel, we came across a cow resting in one of the caves high up on the mountain.

When I observed it closely, I noticed that its mouth was moving continuously—it was chewing the cud or ruminating. In other words, it had eaten some grass earlier and was now regurgitating it, chewing it, swallowing it, then regurgitating it, chewing it and swallowing it again to get the most out of the grass. I know it's not the most appetizing of pictures, but bear with me—I'm coming to something powerful.

If you have been to Mount Arbel, you would know that one side of the mountain is extremely steep. As we carefully descended the precipitous slopes, our bodies were pressed against the side of the mountain at certain points, and some of the guys who were with me were afraid to look down! It is definitely not for the fainthearted and most tourists to Israel would not go down the mountain this way. But I love to go off the beaten track when I am in Israel, and enjoy every facet of the land.

Anyway, that cave was really high up, so I don't know how in the world that cow had gotten up there!

But right there and then, the Lord began to speak to me. He said that many come to church and approach His Word like the other cows grazing at the bottom of the mountain—they simply eat and go. Conversely, this cow that was chewing the cud, ruminating and taking its time to absorb all the nutrients, was kept in a high place—a place of rest, security and perfect calm.

The entire experience was simply amazing. Right there, caressed by the cool winds that swept gently across Mount Arbel, the Lord was teaching me an object lesson on meditating on His Word. He was showing me that when we come to receive His living Word, whether in church on a Sunday or in our quiet moments, He does not want us to simply graze and go. He wants us to take His Word, chew on it and savor it. He wants us to ruminate and meditate upon it. My friend, take a verse or thought from the Lord and chew on it until it bursts forth within you and becomes a revelation in your heart.

Now, biblical meditation involves giving voice to the scripture that you are meditating on. If you look up the word "meditate" in Hebrew (from Psalm 1:2 and Joshua 1:8), it is the word *hagah*, which means "to mutter." So when you meditate on a particular scripture, you should essentially be speaking it to yourself. Speak it out over and over again. Pore over every word and let each one feed and nourish you. Do that and you will be lifted up, elevated into the secret place of the Most High God, far from any form of oppression, anxiety or fear, and enclosed within the embrace of His mighty wings (Psalm 91). That is the power of biblical meditation. I believe with all of my heart that you will experience this rest for your soul as you meditate on the Word and immerse yourself completely in the Lord's unmerited favor for you over the next 100 days.

So what are you waiting for? Let's get started!

The Power Of Looking To Jesus

❖

Today's Scripture

But we all, with unveiled face, beholding as in a mirror the glory of the Lord, are being transformed into the same image from glory to glory, just as by the Spirit of the Lord. —2 Corinthians 3:18

I LOVE TO preach about looking at Jesus and being Christ-occupied instead of being self-occupied. But what is the value of seeing Jesus? How does this put money in your bank account and food on your table? How does this help your children in their studies? Believers who have asked me these questions think that they are being pragmatic, but they don't realize that miracles happen when they keep their eyes on Jesus. Look at what happened to a fisherman called Peter, who was one of Jesus' disciples, in Matthew 14:22–33. When his boat was in the middle of a lake, the most practical thing for a seasoned fisherman to do was to stay in the boat. Science tells you that when you step out into the water, you will sink!

Keep your eyes on Jesus. While it may sound impractical, it is the most powerful thing you can do, and Jesus will cause you to reign over every storm in your life!

But the greatest miracle that Peter experienced happened one night when he stepped out of his boat in the middle of a storm at Jesus' word. That night, the winds were boisterous, but as long as Peter kept his eyes on Jesus, he did the impossible—he walked on water. Jesus was walking on the water and when Peter looked at Jesus, he became like Jesus and did the supernatural. God's Word declares that "we all, with unveiled face, **beholding** as in a mirror the glory of the Lord, are being

transformed into the same image from glory to glory, just as by the Spirit of the Lord."

Beloved, as Jesus is, so are you in this world. When you keep your focus on Jesus, you are transformed into His image from glory to glory. You are transformed by beholding, not by working. When you see that Jesus is above the storms of your life, you will effortlessly rise above those storms. No amount of self-effort could have helped Peter walk on water. When he did, it happened simply because he was looking at Jesus.

Now, observe what happened the moment Peter turned his eyes away from Jesus, and started to look at the wind and the waves around him. In that instance, Peter became natural and he began to sink. Now, let's imagine that there was no storm, no howling winds and no crashing waves that night. Let's imagine that it was a perfectly calm evening and the Sea of Galilee was as still as a mirror without a single ripple on its surface. Could Peter have walked on water then? Of course not!

Walking on water is not something anyone can do whether or not the water is calm. The wind and waves actually made no difference to Peter's ability to walk on the water. The best thing Peter could have done was to keep his eyes on Jesus and not look at the storm. In the same way, instead of looking at how insurmountable your circumstances and challenges are, turn away from them and keep your eyes on Jesus. While it may sound impractical, it is the most powerful thing you can do, and Jesus will cause you to reign over every storm in your life!

Let me share with you a testimony from a lady in our church. She went for a mammogram one morning and the doctors found some lumps in her breast. They told her to return to the clinic in the afternoon so that they could perform further tests to determine if the lumps were cancerous. But this lady was fresh from hearing me teach that as Jesus is, so are we in this world. So before she returned to the clinic for the biopsy, she actually wrote on her medical report, "Does Jesus have lumps in His breast? As He is, so am I in this world." That afternoon, she went for further tests and guess what! The doctors told her that there must have been a mistake—they could find no lumps! Do you know why? Because as He is, so is she!

You have just seen the power of looking to Jesus. If you think that simply looking to Christ is impractical, I am challenging you today to see that it is not. In fact, it is the most practical thing you can ever do. Keep your eyes on Jesus and you will become more and more like Him—full of health, strength, wisdom and life!

❖

Today's Prayer
Father, I know that a man cannot walk on water, whether in stormy or calm conditions. Likewise, whether there are problems in my life or not, I cannot reign in life without Jesus. Apart from Him, I can do NOTHING. Therefore, I ask that You help me keep my eyes on Jesus despite the many things that I have to attend to today. I thank You that as I look to Jesus for all my needs and wants in the midst of every difficulty and challenge, He will place me at the right place at the right time and provide me with every resource I need to experience good success!

Today's Thought
I can walk above my problems when I keep my eyes on Jesus and trust Him.

Today's Reflection On Favor

_____

_____

_____

_____

_____

_____

_____

_____

DAY 2

Meditate On Jesus And Experience Good Success

❖

Today's Scripture

So then faith comes by hearing, and hearing by the word of God [Christ].
—*Romans 10:17*

UNDER THE NEW covenant, we get to meditate on the **person of Jesus** when we meditate on the Word. Jesus is the Word made flesh, and as you meditate on His love for you, on His finished work, on His forgiveness and on His grace, God guarantees that you will have good success.

When you meditate on Jesus, your ways always become prosperous.

You can just take one verse and meditate on Jesus' love for you. For example, you can begin to mutter Psalm 23:1 under your breath: "The Lord is my shepherd, I shall not want." As you meditate on this simple verse, you begin to realize that the Lord **is** (present tense) your shepherd. A shepherd provides for his sheep, feeds them and protects them. Because Jesus is your shepherd, you shall not be in want for anything. You shall not lack wisdom, direction, provision—anything. You begin to see that Jesus is present with you, providing for you, watching out for you, and making sure that you and your family will have more than enough. Now, right at that moment, in that short period of meditating on Jesus, faith is imparted and your heart is encouraged with the reality that Jesus is with you, even when you are facing some challenges.

Whether you are a homemaker, salesperson or business owner, your soul will be nourished and strengthened when you meditate on Jesus. In fact, every time you meditate on God's Word, Jesus will propel you into success without you even realizing it! Without you having to scheme, devise or make all sorts of plans, Jesus will direct your steps, lead you to the place that you are supposed to be at and cause doors of opportunity to supernaturally open wide for you. When you meditate on Jesus, your ways always become prosperous. Now, don't be afraid to use the word "prosperous." It's God's promise in the Bible. When you meditate (mutter) on Jesus day and night, the Bible says that "you will make your way prosperous, and then you will have good success" (Joshua 1:8)!

Some people think that they are prosperous once they have made their first million. But when you examine their lives, you find that somewhere along the way in their struggle to make more and more money, they have lost the very things that are really important. They may have built up an impressive investment portfolio, but their children want nothing to do with them anymore and they have hurt the people who once loved them. That is not true prosperity or good success.

When God blesses you with prosperity, financial blessings are included, but only as a small part of the whole. Good success from Jesus will never take you away from your church. It will never take you away from your loved ones. Most of all, it will never take you away from yourself. You will not wake up one day in the midst of your pursuit of success and find that you no longer know the person looking back at you in the mirror.

My friend, learn to meditate on the person of Jesus. **He** is your good success. When you have Him, you have everything. The Bible tells us that "faith comes by hearing, and hearing by the word of God." The word for "God" here in the original Greek text is *Christos*,[1] referring to Christ. In other words, faith comes by hearing and hearing the Word of **Christ**.

Faith does not come just by hearing the Word of God. Faith comes by hearing the Word of **Jesus** and His finished work. In the same way, meditating on God's Word is about meditating, muttering and hearing about Jesus. This does not mean that you read only the four Gospels of Matthew, Mark, Luke and John. No, every page of the entire Bible from cover to cover points to the person of Jesus!

If you desire to experience good success in your life, then I encourage you to meditate on messages preached by ministries that are all about exalting the person of Jesus, His beauty, His unmerited favor and His perfect work for you on the cross. Listen to new covenant ministries that do not mix law and grace, but which rightly divide the Word of God and preach the unadulterated gospel of Jesus. The more you hear of Jesus and the cross, the more faith will be imparted to you and you will experience good success in your life!

Today's Prayer

Father, I thank You that Your ways are ways of rest. All I have to do is meditate on Jesus and His Word, and He will direct my steps, lead me to the place that I am supposed to be at and cause doors of opportunity to supernaturally open wide for me. Open up Your Words of life to me as I meditate on Jesus, His love for me, His finished work, His forgiveness and His grace.

Today's Thought

When I meditate on Jesus, I will make my way prosperous and have good success.

Today's Reflection On Favor

_____

_____

_____

_____

_____

Jesus Is Interested In Your Success

❖

Today's Scripture

*...Let the Lord be magnified, who has pleasure in the
prosperity of His servant. —Psalm 35:27*

Do you believe that Jesus is interested in your success?

Take a moment to reflect on this.

My friend, I want you to know that Jesus delights in blessing you. It
is His good pleasure to see you blessed in every area of your life! Now,
don't put a limit on His blessings in your life. The blessings of the Lord
are not (as some may erroneously believe) just seen in material things.
Jesus is infinitely interested in your **total** well-being. He is interested in
your family, career, fulfillment in life, marriage, ministry, and boy, does
the list go on!

If it matters to you, it matters to Him!

When it comes to your desires, hopes and dreams, there is no detail
that is too minuscule, minute or insignificant for Jesus. Trust me, if it
matters to you, it matters to Him! Even if you go to Him in prayer to
remove that small pimple on your nose, He is not going to look at you
and reply mockingly, "Hey buddy, don't you know that I've got a whole
universe to run? Come to Me when you have a bigger prayer request."
No way! A thousand times no! Jesus will never ridicule or deride your
concerns as petty. He is never dismissive or condescending. He is not
like some of your so-called "friends," who may delight in poking fun at
your shortcomings. If it bothers you, it "bothers" Him.

You are important to Jesus. Know with full assurance in your heart that Jesus knows you perfectly, and yet accepts and loves you perfectly. When you begin to understand that, you will realize that it is truly that unmerited favor, that favor from Jesus that you know you do not deserve, did not merit and cannot earn for yourself, that will perfect every imperfection and weakness in your life. If you are facing challenges, such as lack in any area, addictions, fears, sicknesses or broken relationships, Jesus' unmerited favor will protect, deliver, prosper, bring restoration to and provide for you. His unmerited favor will transform you into wholeness, and it is the goodness of God, not your striving and self-efforts, that will lead you to live victoriously for His glory.

Today's Prayer

Lord Jesus, thank You for loving me, for being interested in my success and for wanting to bless me in every area of my life. I cast every care on my heart into Your hands. Thank You for Your unmerited favor that gives me wisdom and strength to overcome every problem and to live victoriously today.

Today's Thought

My steps are ordered by the Lord because I am righteous in Him.

Today's Reflection On Favor

_____

_____

_____

_____

_____

_____

_____

_____

_____

It's Not What You Have
But Who You Have

❖

Today's Scripture

*Now Joseph had been taken down to Egypt. And Potiphar,
an officer of Pharaoh, captain of the guard, an Egyptian,
bought him from the Ishmaelites who had taken him down there.
The Lord was with Joseph, and he was a successful man; and he was
in the house of his master the Egyptian. —Genesis 39:1–2*

WOULD YOU CONSIDER the young man Joseph, who was about to be sold
into slavery, "a successful man"?

Of course not!

Yet, God says in His own words that Joseph was a successful man.

God's definition of success is contrary to the world's definition.
Corporate America measures success based on what **you** have done,
what **you** have accomplished and what **you** have accumulated. It is
based entirely on **you** focusing all your time, energy and resources in
meriting titles and collecting accomplishments.

**It is the presence of the Lord in your life that
makes you a success!**

Now, we have witnessed how this self-indulgent accumulation has
led to the subprime crisis, the decimation of investment banks and a
widespread international financial meltdown.

My friend, I want to encourage you to begin to see that the world's
model of success is unstable and built upon a foundation that is

shakable. It may have the appearance of the good life, but it is temporal, and we have all seen for ourselves how the world's transient wealth can dissipate like smoke and easily slip away like the shifting sands in the desert.

From Genesis 39:2, it is clear that success is not **what** you have, but rather **who** you have! Joseph literally had nothing materially, but at the same time, he had everything because the Lord was with him. The material things that you have accumulated or are feverishly trying to amass do not make you a success. It is the presence of the Lord in your life that makes you a success!

We need to learn to stop pursuing things and to start pursuing Him. God sees your relationship with Him as the only thing that you need for every success in your life. I can't imagine starting in a worse place than Joseph. He was completely naked. He had nothing! No bank accounts, no educational qualifications, no natural connections with people of influence, nothing. Thank God the Bible records a picture of Joseph who began with nothing, so that you and I can have hope today. If you think that like Joseph, you have nothing, well, you can start believing in the power of the presence of the Lord in your life. Start looking to Jesus and claim that promise in that scripture for yourself!

Say, "The Lord is with ME, and I am a successful person."

Say it a hundred times if you have to, and begin to see this as your reality. Stick this promise on your mirror, and every morning when you brush your teeth, remind yourself that today, as you go to work, as you go to school, as you start the day caring for your children at home (or do whatever it is that you need to do), the Lord is with you. And because He is with you, YOU ARE ALREADY A SUCCESS! When you have Jesus in your life, you are no longer trying to be a success; you ARE a success!

❖

Today's Prayer

Lord Jesus, I thank You that You are with me, and that You will never leave me nor forsake me. And because I have Your presence in my life, I am already a success! In everything that I need to do today, I know that You are with me to help me succeed at it.

Today's Thought

Because the Lord is with me, I am a successful person.

Today's Reflection On Favor

_____

_____

_____

_____

_____

_____

_____

_____

_____

_____

_____

_____

_____

_____

_____

_____

_____

DAY 5

Jesus, Our Perfect Hero

❖

Today's Scripture

*His mouth is most sweet, yes, he is altogether lovely. This is my beloved,
and this is my friend, O daughters of Jerusalem! —Song of Solomon 5:16*

JESUS IS SOMEONE whom you can be completely real with. You can hang
out with Him and be yourself, with no pretense and no play-acting. Jesus
is ever-loving toward you and you can talk to Him about anything. He
enjoys conversing with you about your dreams, aspirations and hopes.
He wants to heal you of things in your past that you may be struggling
with. He is interested in your present challenges. He wants to weep with
you when you are down and rejoice with you in all your victories.

Jesus is someone whom you can be completely real with.

Jesus is love and tenderness personified. Be careful not to confuse
His tenderness with the effeminate and weak images that you have seen
depicted in some traditional paintings of Him. He is tenderness and
strength wrapped up in one. He is meekness and majesty, manhood
and deity, velvet and steel. You see, sometimes, when we attempt to
be assertive and strong, we bulldoze over people's feelings and end
up hurting them with our words. When we attempt to be tender, we
overdose on niceness and reduce ourselves to doormats to be taken
advantage of by others.

Let's turn away from ourselves and look at Jesus. He could sternly
force a pack of scheming Pharisees to back off in one instance,
challenging them by saying, "He who is without sin among you, let him
throw a stone at her first" (John 8:7). In the very next moment, this

same Jesus could look straight into the eyes of a broken woman caught in adultery, and with compassion resonating deeply in His voice, ask her, "Woman, where are those accusers of yours? Has no one condemned you? Neither do I condemn you; go and sin no more" (John 8:10–11).

This is our God!

In one moment, a tired Jesus could be fast asleep in a wind-swept fisherman's boat, oblivious to the rough Galilean waters crashing against the hapless vessel. But in the very next moment, you see Him staring unflinchingly at the lashing waves, His well-toned carpenter's arms raised to the sky. With His single declaration of absolute authority over heaven and earth, the waves submitted and calmed instantaneously into a placid mirror of stillness (Mark 4:37–39).

Jesus is 100 percent Man and at the same time 100 percent God. As Man, He understands and identifies with all that you have gone through, are going through and will ever go through in this life. But as a loving God, all His power, authority and resources are on your side. Beloved, whatever you are facing today, let your heart rest easy in His perfect love for you.

❖

Today's Prayer

Father, help me to keep my eyes on Jesus, the one who is altogether lovely. For my sake, Lord Jesus, You became a man so that today, You understand everything I'm going through and every emotion I feel. Thank You, Jesus, for not condemning me, but loving me always and for reassuring me today that I have the presence of the all-loving and all-powerful God-Man in my life to help and prosper me in every area of life.

Today's Thought
Jesus understands and identifies with all that I have gone through,
am going through and will ever go through in this life.

Today's Reflection On Favor

_____

_____

_____

_____

_____

_____

_____

_____

_____

_____

_____

_____

_____

_____

_____

_____

_____

_____

_____

_____

Saving You Is God's Job Description

❖

Today's Scripture

But while he thought about these things, behold, an angel of the Lord appeared to him in a dream, saying, "Joseph, son of David, do not be afraid to take to you Mary your wife, for that which is conceived in her is of the Holy Spirit. And she will bring forth a Son, and you shall call His name Jesus, for He will save His people from their sins."
—Matthew 1:20–21

THE NAME "JESUS" is *Yeshua* in Hebrew, which contains an abbreviation for *Yahweh*, the name of God in Hebrew. So the name "Jesus" literally means "*Yahweh* is our Savior" or "The Lord is our Savior"! What a beautiful name!

Jesus is your Savior!

Every time you call the name of Jesus, the name that is above every other name, you are calling God Himself to save you. Saving you is Jesus' job description! Whatever the challenge or circumstance, whatever crisis you are in—physically, financially or emotionally—you can call on the name of Jesus and Almighty God Himself will save you!

My friend, you can take time to know the names of God, which He revealed under the old covenant, such as *Elohim, El Shaddai, El Elyon, Jehovah-Jireh, Jehovah-Rophe* and *Jehovah-Nissi*. You can do a complete study on the names of God. I am not against that at all. I teach on the names of God in my church as well, but all these names will mean nothing to you if you don't know that God Almighty Himself, Jesus, wants to save you first from all your sins, then from all your challenges.

God can be all powerful, but if you are not confident that He is interested in your success, His power would mean nothing to you. So, you don't have to memorize all the names of God from the old covenant. What you need is a full revelation that Jesus, in the new covenant, is your *Savior*! What is Tiger Woods famous for? Golf! What is David Beckham famous for? Soccer! (He's also famous for product endorsements!) What is Jesus famous for? Saving you!

What do you need saving from today? See Him in your situation, rescuing, protecting and providing for you!

❖

Today's Prayer

Lord Jesus, because You are my mighty Savior, there is no challenge or circumstance that can successfully defeat me. Thank You for saving me from my sins and from every challenge that besets me today. I receive Your wisdom, protection and provision to deliver me from and prosper me in every difficult circumstance I have to deal with today.

Today's Thought

Jesus has saved me from my sins and His power is available to save me from any and every challenge in my life.

Today's Reflection On Favor

_____

_____

_____

_____

_____

_____

_____

_____

God Is Able And Willing

❖

Today's Scripture

And behold, a leper came and worshiped Him, saying, "Lord, if You are willing, You can make me clean." Then Jesus put out His hand and touched him, saying, "I am willing; be cleansed." Immediately his leprosy was cleansed. —Matthew 8:2–3

ALL CHRISTIANS PROBABLY believe that God has the **power** to bless, heal, protect, prosper and make someone a success. However, we know that not all Christians believe that God is **willing** to do all that for them. Matthew 8:1–3 records the story of a leper who came to Jesus for healing. He said, "Lord, if You are willing, You can make me clean." The leper did not doubt Jesus' ability to heal him, but he was unsure if Jesus was **willing** to heal **him**, a leper who was ostracized by all. In other words, he believed in God's omnipotence, but was not sure if God's heart was one of love and unmerited favor toward him. I am sure that you know believers who are like that. They may believe in God's power, but they are unsure of God's heart toward them. They know that God can, but they are not sure if He is willing.

Whatever breakthrough you are believing Jesus for, He says to you, "I AM WILLING."

This is one of the biggest tragedies in the church today. When these believers hear testimonies of believers being healed by the Lord, they are unsure if God is also willing to heal them. When they read praise reports of the Lord blessing others with promotions and financial blessings, they privately question if God is also willing to do the same for them. They wonder what these people **did** to get their blessings.

More tragically, they look at their own lives, imperfections and failings, and start to disqualify themselves from receiving God's blessings. They think, "Why would God bless me? Look at what I've done. I am so undeserving." Instead of having faith to believe God for their breakthroughs, they feel too condemned to be able to believe in God's goodness and receive anything good from Him.

My friend, don't be like that leper who completely misread Jesus! Let's see how Jesus responded to him. This is important because it would be the same response that Jesus would give you if you approached Him today.

Matthew 8:3 records that "Jesus put out His hand and touched him, saying, 'I am willing; be cleansed.'" Can you see how personal Jesus' ministry is? He did not touch every person that He healed. At times, He simply spoke and the sick were healed. But in this case, Jesus stretched out His hand and touched the leper tenderly. I believe that Jesus did this to heal him not just of his leprosy, but also of the emotional scars that he had received from years of rejection.

Leprosy was a highly contagious disease and the law forbade lepers from coming into contact with anyone. This meant that for years, this leper had been shunned by everyone who saw his condition, even his own family members. He probably stank of decaying flesh and neglect, and his appearance must have been repulsive.

But without flinching, Jesus touched him, giving him the first human touch he had since he contracted the disease. The Bible tells us that immediately, his leprosy was cleansed and the man received his healing.

Jesus is the same yesterday, today and forever (Hebrews 13:8). Whatever breakthrough you are believing Him for, He says to you, "I AM WILLING." Don't doubt His heart of love for you any longer. Stop being occupied by your own disqualifications and be completely absorbed in His love and grace (unmerited favor) toward you!

❖

Today's Prayer

Father, thank You for recording the story of the leper in Your Word for me. It shows me that when it comes to healing and all the other blessings that Jesus died to give me, You CAN and ARE WILLING to give them to me. I thank You that my imperfections and failings don't disqualify me from Your blessings because the blood of Jesus has already qualified me. His sacrifice unleashes Your unmerited favor and blessings upon me! Thank You for the blessings that You have lined up for me to walk in today.

Today's Thought

God can and He IS WILLING to do it for ME!

Today's Reflection On Favor

_____

_____

_____

_____

_____

_____

_____

_____

_____

_____

_____

_____

_____

_____

DAY 8

God's Love For You Is Personal, Detailed And In-Depth

❖

Today's Scripture

Therefore humble yourselves under the mighty hand of God, that He may exalt you in due time, casting all your care upon Him, for He cares for you. —1 Peter 5:6–7

THERE ARE MANY believers today who don't cast their cares upon the Lord. I believe that it is because they don't have a revelation that He cares for them. Look at what His Word says: "casting all your care upon Him, for **He cares for you**." Unless you have absolute confidence that Jesus cares for you, you will not cast your cares upon Him. Just think, would you call upon the help of a relative or friend in your time of need if you were not confident that the person would respond to your call? Jesus cares for you. When you call upon Him, know that you have His fullest attention with all of heaven's resources backing you up!

God is vitally and intensely involved in the day-to-day minute details of your life.

Maybe you are thinking right now, "Well, I am sure that Jesus has more important things to do than to bother with my problem." Hang on. By saying that, you have just shown that you don't really believe that Jesus cares for you. Now, let's see what the Bible says: "But the very hairs of your head are all numbered. Do not fear therefore; you are of more value than many sparrows" (Luke 12:7).

I love and care for my sweet daughter, Jessica. But as much as I adore her and care for her well-being, I have never, not once, counted the number of strands of hair on her head! She does not know how great a blessing she has been to me. I love to kiss her, smell her hair and hug her tightly. Yet, in all my great love for her, I have never taken the time to count the number of strands of hair on her head in all these years!

But do you know that your heavenly Father numbers the hairs on your head? I really hope that you are beginning to catch the heart of Jesus and not generalize His love for you. His love for you is all-encompassing. If He cares enough to keep track of the hairs on your head, is there anything too small for Him that you cannot talk to Him about?

God's love for you is infinitely detailed. Jesus said that not one sparrow falls to the ground apart from the Father's will (Matthew 10:29). Are you not of more value than a sparrow? Is God a God who winds the clock and leaves it alone to tick until Jesus comes back? Is He only involved with major events in the world? Is He only involved in significant events in our lives like our salvation, or is He vitally and intensely involved in the day-to-day minute details of your life? What do you think? The Bible says that He calls His own sheep by name (John 10:3, 14). My friend, His love for you is personal, detailed and in-depth! Your heavenly Father wants you to involve Him even in the smallest, most mundane matters of your life, and see His unmerited favor surround you, protect you and lead you to good success.

❖

Today's Prayer

Father, thank You for loving me in such a personal, detailed and in-depth way. Right now, I cast every care and concern that I have in my heart for myself and my family into Your hands. I ask that You take care of them for me and that You direct my paths. I refuse to fret and worry about any of my problems anymore because they are in Your hands. Instead, I choose to thank You for Your awesome answers!

Today's Thought

God cares for me intensely and His love for me is personal, detailed and in-depth.

Today's Reflection On Favor

_____

_____

_____

_____

_____

_____

_____

_____

_____

_____

_____

_____

_____

_____

_____

_____

_____

_____

Jesus Is Immanuel, The Almighty God With Us

❖

Today's Scripture

So all this was done that it might be fulfilled which was spoken by the Lord through the prophet, saying: "Behold, the virgin shall be with child, and bear a Son, and they shall call His name Immanuel," which is translated, "God with us." —Matthew 1:22–23

DID YOU KNOW that Jesus' name is not just Jesus? His name is also **Immanuel**, meaning the Almighty God is with us. How comforting it is to know that our awesome Almighty God, who is also our loving Father, is always with us!

A precious brother shared with me that even as a believer years ago, he had a problem with alcohol, and every night he would be out drinking to the point that he could not even remember how he got home the next day. He tried everything he could to stop drinking, but failed repeatedly.

When Almighty God is with you, good things will happen in you, around you and through you.

One day, he went out with some friends for a game of squash. After the game, he laid down on the ground to rest. As he was resting, he felt Jesus' presence come upon him and in that very moment, the Lord broke his addiction to alcohol and totally removed his desire to drink!

Today, this brother whom the Lord delivered from alcoholism is a key leader in my church. Isn't it just like God to take the weak things of the world to confound the mighty, and the foolish things of the world to confound the wise?

You know, all our struggling, willpower, discipline and self-effort cannot do what the presence of the Lord can do in an instant. And who is to say that as we are talking about Jesus now, His presence will not take away something that is destructive in your life?

You see, you are transformed not by struggling. You are transformed by beholding Jesus and believing that He loves you and wants to save you.

Now, what does it mean to say "God with us"? We must understand it the same way the Hebrew people would have understood it. There is something beautiful here—this is the secret of Immanuel! The Jewish mind understands that when the Lord is **with you**, you become successful in every endeavor. Don't just take my word for it. Look through the chronicles of Jewish history. The Bible records that whenever the Lord was **with them** in battle, the children of Israel were never defeated, and every military campaign ended in overwhelming success.

In fact, in the battle for Jericho, the city was theirs with just a shout (Joshua 6:20)! Why? The Lord was with them. Even in battles when they were outnumbered, they triumphed because the Lord was with them. It is no different for you today. When the Bible says that Jesus is with you, He is with you to help you, assist you, turn things around for you and make good things happen for you. He is not with you, as some wrongly believe, to condemn, judge or find fault! When Almighty God is **with you**, good things will happen **in you**, **around you** and **through you**. Expect this to happen to you today!

❖

Today's Prayer

Lord Jesus, I thank You that You are always with me. Help me remember that it is not my willpower, self-efforts or discipline that will give me victory over temptations and addictions, but Your presence in my life. Thank You for the good things that will happen to me and for me and my loved ones because of Your presence in my life.

Today's Thought

Victory comes not by my willpower, but Jesus' presence.

Today's Reflection On Favor

_____

_____

_____

_____

_____

_____

_____

_____

_____

_____

_____

_____

_____

_____

_____

_____

_____

_____

_____

_____

_____

_____

DAY 10

God Is Not Present To Find Fault With You

Today's Scripture

In all your ways acknowledge Him, and He shall direct your paths.
—*Proverbs 3:6*

SOMETHING VERY UNIQUE and precious happens when you see that the Lord is with you. Trust the Lord to open your eyes to see Him in your situation, and the more you see Him, the more He manifests Himself. If you are in the midst of committing to an important business agreement, I assure you that if you can see the Lord there with you, His wisdom will flow through you, and He will give you supernatural insight to locate any loopholes, details or exit clauses that are missing from that contract that you are about to sign.

God's presence is with you to direct you, guide you, lead you into becoming more like Christ, and to make you a success in every endeavor you undertake.

Once you involve Jesus and acknowledge His presence, you will sense Him intervening in any decision you are about to make, through the absence or presence of His peace. Sometimes, everything can appear to be in order on the surface, but somehow, you may sense a discomfort rising up in you every time you think about your decision. My advice to you would be to not rush into it. You see, once you have involved the Lord, the lack of peace that you feel is often His leading to protect you. You can even be in the midst of an argument with your spouse, but the moment you become conscious of the Lord's presence, your words will change. Somehow, there will be a supernatural restraint that you know is not from yourself. That is also the Lord!

Beloved, it is important for you to eradicate the notion that the Lord is present to **find fault** with you. You may have been raised in an environment where your parents were constantly picking on your faults and pointing out your mistakes, but don't project this characteristic onto the Lord. God knows every idiosyncrasy about you, yet He loves you perfectly because He sees you through the lens of the cross, where His Son has removed every failing from your life. This means that even your current argument with your spouse is washed by the blood of Jesus.

The Lord's presence is with you not to judge you or smack you on the head with a giant bat the moment you fail. No, my friend, His presence is with you to direct you, guide you, lead you into becoming more like Christ, and to make you a success in every endeavor you undertake.

Today's Prayer

Lord Jesus, I am so glad to know that You are with me not to find fault with me, but to encourage me, guide me and help me experience good success. Help me to always involve You and acknowledge Your presence in whatever decision I am making. Today, I look forward to seeing Your presence manifesting as supernatural wisdom and discernment in me to do what is right and full of life.

Today's Thought

God knows all my idiosyncrasies and weaknesses, yet He doesn't condemn me but loves me perfectly because of Jesus.

Today's Reflection On Favor

_____

_____

_____

_____

DAY 11

It's Not The End When The Lord Is With You

❖

Today's Scripture

And his master [Potiphar] saw that the Lord was with him [Joseph] and that the Lord made all he did to prosper in his hand. —*Genesis 39:3*

Do YOU KNOW of anyone who is in a worse situation than Joseph when he stood naked in an Egyptian market, waiting to be sold as a slave? His whole world appeared to have collapsed around him. Just a few days earlier, he was in his father's embrace but now, his own brothers had betrayed him. All that he owned had been stripped from him. He was reduced to nothing more than a slave in a foreign land.

When God's presence is made manifest in your life, that's when His glory shines forth through you!

Was this the end of Joseph? In the natural scheme of things, it sure looked like it was. But even with the odds stacked up against Joseph, the Lord was far from finished. Even in this dire situation, the Lord was with Joseph, and at this dark and bleak juncture in Joseph's life, the Lord called him a successful man (Genesis 39:1–2)! Remember, it is not what you have. It is **who** you have that makes all the difference.

"How can the Lord make a young slave with not a single cent or possession to his name succeed?"

Well, let's continue with Joseph's story. Genesis 39:3 tells us, "And his master [Potiphar] saw that the Lord was with him [Joseph] and that the Lord made all he did to prosper in his hand." This is a powerful statement and it offers a promise that you can believe Jesus for, in every

28

area of your life. Can you imagine every project, assignment and even errand that you undertake becoming prosperous? Your hands become hands of blessing.

You touch your family members and they are blessed. Your company may be struggling to manage a difficult project, but once it is placed in your hands, the project becomes blessed. You become a blessing waiting to happen to someone, waiting to happen to something, everywhere you go!

Now, how will this happen? The Lord Jesus will make it happen when you depend on Him in the same way that Joseph depended on Him. Joseph had nothing. He could not trust in his skills or experience (he had never been a slave), nor could he trust in his natural connections (his father was out of the picture because he believed that Joseph had been killed by a wild animal). All Joseph had was the Lord's presence, and he depended on the Lord to manifest His presence, His power and His glory through him!

That's what you and I need—a manifestation of His presence in everything that we do! You see, it is one thing to have His presence (all Christians have His presence because they have accepted Him as their personal Lord and Savior), but when His presence is made manifest in your life, that's when His glory shines forth through you!

Don't forget that Joseph's master, Potiphar, was not a believer in God. He was an Egyptian who worshipped idols. Yet, when the manifested presence of the Lord shone gloriously through the work of Joseph's hands, even this unbelieving heathen could see the tangible results of the Lord's special anointing, power and blessing upon Joseph's life. Potiphar marveled and could not but acknowledge that the Lord was with Joseph, and that "the Lord made all he did to prosper in his hand."

Now, isn't it interesting that Potiphar did not merely conclude that Joseph was a good worker? Instead, Potiphar could see that it was not Joseph's skills, but rather, his God who was prospering all that Joseph set his hands to. Genesis 39:3 tells us that "the Lord made all he did to prosper in his hand." This could not have been "spiritual discernment" on Potiphar's part—he was not a believer and had no spiritual discernment when it came to the things of God. So this tells me that Potiphar must have witnessed tangible results that were really out of this world. He must have seen results that were so spectacular that he knew they were beyond that of an ordinary human being!

Perhaps Potiphar ordered Joseph to dig new wells for his household and every well that Joseph dug yielded water even in the midst of a drought. Perhaps the field that Joseph tended yielded crops that were shockingly bigger than the crops in the surrounding fields. Perhaps Potiphar saw how Joseph called upon his God when the children in the house were suffering from some epidemic in the land, and they were all healed. Whatever the case was, Potiphar knew that the prosperous results he had witnessed were not a result of Joseph's natural abilities. They had to be due to the fact that the Lord was with Joseph, and God made all he did to prosper in his hand. Isn't that beautiful? My friend, God wants to do the same in your life today. See Him leading and blessing you, and increasing your effectiveness today!

❖

Today's Prayer

Father, despite the negative circumstances in my life, thank You for reminding me that it is not the end for me. I will be successful because You are with me. Your unmerited favor upon me will cause the work of my hands to prosper and yield supernaturally good results! I shall see all that You have put in my hands abundantly blessed!

Today's Thought

I can have success beyond my natural abilities and in spite of any negative environment because the Lord is with me.

Today's Reflection On Favor

_____

_____

_____

_____

_____

_____

_____

_____

_____

_____

_____

_____

_____

_____

_____

_____

_____

_____

_____

_____

DAY 12

Start Your Day With Jesus

❖

Today's Scripture

It is good to give thanks to the Lord, and to sing praises to Your name,
O Most High; to declare Your lovingkindness in the morning,
and Your faithfulness every night. —Psalm 92:1–2

Do YOU KNOW that God has promised that no weapon formed against you shall prosper (Isaiah 54:17)? Now, He did not promise that weapons would not be formed against you. He promised that even if weapons were formed against you, they would not hurt or defeat you.

Start your day with Jesus—practicing His presence, committing your plans to Him and trusting Him for His unmerited favor, wisdom and strength for the day.

There are all kinds of weapons formed against humanity, especially in these last days. Just think of the many kinds of deadly viruses, sicknesses and diseases in the world. When you turn on the television and watch the news, all you seem to hear about are wars, unrest, disasters, financial collapses, violence, unemployment, famines and new strains of deadly viruses. It is amazing how many people wake up in the morning, and the first thing that they do is grab the newspapers and read bad news before heading to work. Then, just before they go to bed, they watch the news!

Now, please understand that I am not against reading the newspapers or watching the news, or watching television for that matter. But I want to encourage you to start your day with Jesus instead, practicing His presence, acknowledging Him, committing your plans to Him and trusting Him for His unmerited favor, wisdom and strength for the day.

Remember to be like Joseph in the Bible. The Lord was with Joseph and he was a successful man! Your success does not come as a result of you being updated about the latest virus or you being cued in to the latest disaster. No, your success will come as a result of your being tuned in to the presence of Jesus in your life!

There are many people in my church who start the day each morning by partaking of the Holy Communion, not as a ritual, but as a time to remember Jesus and the power of His cross. They look to Jesus for His strength, receiving His divine life for their physical bodies as they partake of the bread. They renew their consciousness of their free gift of righteousness purchased by the blood of Jesus on the cross as they partake of the cup. What a way to start the day!

I have also come to realize that the last thought before you go to sleep is very important. I have tried this before and you can try it too—go to bed thinking about Jesus, giving thanks to Him for the day. You can also meditate on one of His promises, such as the one found in Isaiah 54:17. Just say, "Thank You, Father. Your Word declares that no weapon formed against me shall prosper!" Most times, I wake up feeling rejuvenated, energized and refreshed even though I did not sleep for many hours.

Conversely, if I go to bed with what I have just heard on the news swirling in my mind, I could sleep many more hours than usual, but still wake up feeling fatigued. Sometimes I even get a headache. Have you been there before? Well, you don't have to experience that again. Sandwich your day with the presence of Jesus. Start the day with Him, enjoy Him during the day and end the day with Him on your mind!

❖

Today's Prayer

*Lord Jesus, thank You for Your presence with me today. Help me to
be more conscious of Your unmerited favor toward me than of bad news
that people are concerned about. Today, I commit all my plans to You,
knowing that Your unmerited favor, wisdom and strength are
always with me to prosper me and give me good success.*

Today's Thought

I'm going to sandwich this day with the presence of Jesus.

Today's Reflection On Favor

_____

Practice Jesus' Presence
And See His Power

❖

Today's Scripture

But the Lord is with me as a mighty, awesome One. Therefore my persecutors will stumble, and will not prevail... —Jeremiah 20:11

Do you know that the best time to thank Jesus for His presence is when you don't "feel" His presence? When it comes to the presence of Jesus, don't go by your feelings. Feelings can be deceptive. Go by His promise that He is Immanuel—God with us!

Feelings aren't based on truth. God's Word is truth!

Have you heard the story of a groom who approached his pastor almost immediately after his wedding ceremony? He went up to his pastor and said, "Pastor, can I talk to you for a second?"

"Sure," the pastor replied.

The groom said, "You know what, I don't **feel** married."

The pastor grabbed him by the collar and growled, "Listen, boy. You ARE married whether you feel it or not, understand? Just take it by faith that you are married!"

You see, my friend, you can't go by your feelings. You go by the truth and the truth is this: God promised, "I will never leave you nor forsake you." So the best time to practice His presence is precisely when you **feel** like Jesus is 100,000 miles away. Remember that feelings aren't based on truth. God's Word is truth!

Soon after I graduated from high school, I took on a part-time job to teach in an elementary school where I was placed in charge of a class of 10-year-olds. I remember one day, when I was practicing His presence, I knelt down in my living room and prayed, "Lord, I just thank You that You are always with me." As I was on my knees, the Lord told me to pray specifically for one of the girls in my class who had been absent from school that day.

Now, it is very common for kids to miss class now and then for various reasons, and I had never been led by the Lord to pray specifically for any of them. This girl was the first! The Lord told me very clearly to pray for His protection to be over this girl and to cover her with His precious blood.

The next day, there was a big commotion in the school and I found out that the girl had been kidnapped by a notorious serial killer that very afternoon when the Lord had told me to pray for her. The killer, Adrian Lim, had kidnapped several children to be offered up as sacrifices to the devil. He believed that Satan would give him power when he offered the blood of these children to him.

Over the next couple of days, this girl from my class was all over our national media because she had been miraculously released. Sadly, she was the only girl released. All the other kidnapped children had been brutally murdered.

When she returned to class, I asked her how she came to be freed. She told me that her kidnapper was "praying" over her when suddenly he stopped and told her, "The gods do not want you." She was quickly released that evening. Of course, you and I know why the "gods" didn't want her—she was covered and protected by Jesus' blood!

Listen to what I am saying here. In America today and around the world, the devil is trying to destroy a new generation because he is afraid that the young people of the new millennium are going to take over the world for Jesus. That is why we have to cover our children with Jesus' protection.

I am sharing all this with you because I want you to see the importance and power of practicing His presence. As a teacher during that time, my class was my responsibility, just like my congregation is my responsibility today. Think with me: How in the world, with my finite knowledge and intelligence, could I have known that one of my students was in grave danger? It is not possible! But because the Lord, who knows all things, was with me, He enabled me to make a difference in my student's life.

Similarly, whatever role or vocation you are in, whether you are a schoolteacher, business leader or homemaker, I want you to know that Jesus is with you and He wants to make you a success. Now, remember, all this happened to me before I became a full-time pastor, so please don't think that this unmerited favor from Jesus is only for pastors. Beloved, His unmerited favor is for you. The Lord Immanuel is **with you**.

❖

Today's Prayer

Father, I thank You that You are always with me. You will never leave me nor forsake me. And because Your presence is always with me, I am always protected, blessed, accurate and effective in all that I need to do and in every place and role I find myself in.

Today's Thought

Whether I feel it or not, the Lord Immanuel is with me right now.

Today's Reflection On Favor

_____

_____

_____

_____

_____

_____

DAY 14

Your Fears And Anxieties Dissipate In God's Presence

❖

Today's Scripture

The mountains melt like wax at the presence of the Lord...
—Psalm 97:5

No MATTER WHERE you are, the Lord is with you. Even in the midst of your fears, while you are alone in your room, He is there with you. The moment you begin to be aware of His presence and cultivate His presence, all your fears, anxieties and worries will melt like butter on a hot day, or as the psalmist David puts it, "The mountains melt like wax at the presence of the Lord..."

It takes the presence of the Lord to keep you free from worry.

You cannot psych yourself out of fear nor can you psych yourself out of worry. You can't just tell yourself, "Come on, stop worrying. There is nothing to worry about." It just doesn't work. The debt will still be staring you in your face and your problems will still be as insurmountable as ever no matter how hard you try to psych yourself up. That is what the world is trying to do, but it does not work. It takes the presence of the Lord to keep you free from worry.

Jesus is not asking you to psych yourself up and live in a state of denial. No way! He is saying to you, "In the midst of your affliction, I am your shield. I am your defender. I am your fortress. I am your refuge. I am your supply. I am your healing. I am your provider. I am your peace. I am your joy. I am your wisdom. I am your strength. I am the glory and the lifter of your head!" (Psalm 3:3). Amen! He is not asking you to pretend that the facts are not there. He wants you to realize that HE IS THERE WITH YOU!

When you know that He is with you and for you, and you put your problems in His mighty hands, you will begin to get a more accurate evaluation of just how "big" your problems are. When they were in your hands, the weight and burden of your problems may have crushed you. But when you involve Jesus, the once-monumental problems become microscopic against the largeness of His love and goodness toward you!

Today, as you consider all that you need to do and the expectations placed on you, see Jesus there with you. He is your supply, wisdom, peace and strength.

❖

Today's Prayer
Father, I acknowledge the fact that I cannot psych away my fears and worries. Therefore, I cast all my cares into Your hands, to the one who is my shield, my fortress, my healing, my provision, my peace, my wisdom and my strength. Thank You for Your grace and for taking care of all my problems today.

Today's Thought
Once you cast your monumental problems to Jesus, they become microscopic in His mighty hands.

Today's Reflection On Favor

_____

_____

_____

_____

_____

_____

_____

DAY 15

God Is On Your Side Today!

❖

Today's Scripture

If God is for us, who can be against us? —Romans 8:31

Romans 8:31 contains a powerful rhetorical question and I encourage you to memorize it. Unfortunately, there are still some believers today wondering, "Is God really for me?" Well, my friend, the Word of God does NOT say "**maybe** God is for us" or "**hopefully**, God is for us." It simply says, "If God is for us, who can be against us?" Indeed, when God is for you, what opposition can succeed against you? When God Himself fights for you, defends you and vindicates you, what adversity or adversary can stand against you? There are none! Hallelujah!

God is for you today because of the blood of the perfect Lamb—Jesus Christ.

"But Pastor Prince, how did God come to be on our side? Even though I am a Christian today, I still fail and fall short of God's holy standards. I still lose my temper on the road now and then, and from time to time, I still get angry with my wife and kids. Why should God be on my side when I fail? Don't you know that God's holy?"

All great questions. Let me tell you why God is on our side. The answer is found at the cross. The blood that Jesus Christ, the Son of God, shed on the cross put God on your side. Today, God can be for you even when you fail because Jesus' blood has washed you whiter than snow!

Have you seen Cecil DeMille's movie, *The Ten Commandments*, or the animation, *The Prince Of Egypt*? Do you remember what happened on the night of the Passover? The children of Israel put the blood of the lamb on their doorposts. What did the blood do? The blood put God on their side! None of the families who had applied blood on their doorposts had to fear the death of their firstborn children.

Now, think about this for a moment. Were the firstborn children of Israel spared that night because of their perfect behavior and conduct, or were they spared because of the blood of the lamb? Of course, it was because of the blood of the lamb!

In the same way, God does not bless you, as a new covenant believer, based on your perfect behavior and conduct. He is **for you** today because of the blood of the perfect Lamb—Jesus Christ. That is why as believers today, we don't have to fight for ourselves. I like to say it this way: "If God is for us, who can come successfully against us?"

Always remember that God is on your side today because of Jesus' blood. His holiness and righteousness that men are afraid of are now on your side because of Jesus' blood. His unmerited favor is on your side and all of heaven's resources are yours because of Jesus' blood! Now, who can come successfully against you? No sickness, no disease, no creditor, no evil accusation, no gossip—no weapon formed against you, can come successfully against you (Isaiah 54:17)!

❖

Today's Prayer

Father, I thank You that You are on my side and You are for me today because of the blood of Jesus shed for me. Your holiness, righteousness and favor are on my side and all of heaven's resources are mine not because of my goodness, but because of Jesus' blood alone. Help me remember that because His blood avails for me forever, You are forever for me and for my well-being.

Today's Thought

If God is for me because of Jesus' blood, then no one—nothing—can come successfully against me.

Today's Reflection On Favor

_____

_____

_____

_____

_____

_____

_____

_____

_____

_____

_____

_____

_____

_____

_____

_____

_____

_____

_____

_____

_____

There Is Just Something Special About You

❖

Today's Scripture

But you are a chosen generation, a royal priesthood, a holy nation, His own special people, that you may proclaim the praises of Him who called you out of darkness into His marvelous light. —*1 Peter 2:9*

IT IS THE Lord's manifested presence, His glorious power working in your heart and through your hands that will cause everything you touch to prosper with the Jesus-kind of results. In fact, even your harshest critic will have to conclude that the Lord is with you and is prospering the work of your hands!

Because Jesus is with you, expect good success in everything that you do!

Beloved, stop looking at your outward circumstances or the position you are in. Whether your employer is a believer or not, Jesus can make ALL that you do prosper when you depend on His unmerited favor in your career! And believe me, when that begins to happen, your employer will sit up and notice that there is something special about you. You will stand out in a crowd! Remember that the same Lord who was with Joseph is with you today. His name is Jesus and because Jesus is with you, you can expect good success in everything that you do!

For example, when you are placed over a sales project, believe that your sales team will hit record levels of sales never achieved before in your organization. When you are overseeing the finances of a company, believe that you will find legal ways to help your company save on operating expenses and increase its cash flow like never before. When you are placed in a business development role, believe that Jesus will cause doors that have always been closed to your company to be opened to you because of His unmerited favor upon your life. Perhaps your company is just a small IT start-up in the Silicon Valley, but for some reason, all the big boys in Microsoft, IBM and Oracle like you. They can't put their finger on it, but there is just something special about you that makes them compete to find ways to collaborate with you, leaving you spoiled for choice!

Perhaps you are a homemaker. You can also expect Jesus' presence in your life to give you favor with your children. Instead of constantly resisting and arguing with you, they will find you and your words irresistible. God can increase your influence over them.

My friend, that's the unmerited favor of God in action. In the natural, you may be unqualified and inexperienced, but remember that all your disqualifications exist in the realm of the natural. You, beloved, live and operate in the supernatural realm! The Lord Jesus is with you 100 percent. You are a successful person in the Lord's eyes and as you depend on Him, He will cause everything that your hands touch to prosper.

❖

Today's Prayer

Lord Jesus, I thank You that I have favor with my bosses, colleagues and clients because You are with me. And because of Your presence in my life, I know that I cannot help but excel in my projects and assignments. I choose not to be mindful of my lack of qualifications and experience. Instead, I expect to see good success in my relationships with people and in everything that I need to do today.

Today's Thought
I am special because Jesus is with me!

Today's Reflection On Favor

_____

_____

_____

_____

_____

_____

_____

_____

_____

_____

_____

_____

_____

_____

_____

_____

_____

_____

_____

_____

_____

DAY 17

Without Jesus, We Cannot
Without Us, He Will Not

Today's Scripture

*I am the vine, you are the branches. He who abides in Me, and I in him,
bears much fruit; for without Me you can do nothing. —John 15:5*

IN MORE THAN two decades of ministry, I have learned this from the Lord:
Without Him, we cannot. Without us, He will not. What this simply
means is that we need to recognize the fact that if we do not depend on
Jesus, there can be no real, long-lasting and abiding success—without
Him, we cannot. The Bible tells us that unless the Lord builds the house,
we labor in vain (Psalm 127:1). Believers who want to experience His
success need to recognize this truth and begin to depend on Jesus and
Jesus alone.

**If we do not depend on Jesus, there can be no real,
long-lasting and abiding success.**

There are some believers who may not articulate it, but in their hearts,
they believe that without Jesus, they can still succeed. By believing
and acting on this, they fall from the high place of God's grace (His
unmerited favor) back into the law, back into trying to merit and deserve
success by their own efforts. God's Word tells us, "For if you are trying
to make yourselves right with God by keeping the law, you have been
cut off from Christ! You have fallen away from God's grace [unmerited
favor]" (Galatians 5:4 NLT).

These are strong words of warning. Once you start depending on
your own merits and efforts to deserve God's favor, you are back under

the system of the law. You are cut off from Christ and have fallen from the place of having His unmerited favor work in your life. Don't misunderstand me, Jesus is still with you (He will never leave you nor forsake you [Hebrews 13:5]), but by depending on your self-efforts, you effectively cut off His unmerited favor in your life.

So what do I mean when I say, "Without us, He will not"? Well, Jesus is a gentleman. He will not force His unmerited favor and success down your throat. He needs you to allow Him to work in your life. He waits patiently for you to trust Him. He waits patiently for you to depend on His unmerited favor, the way Joseph trusted and depended wholly on the Lord's presence, until His manifested presence took over, and His glory radiated from everything that Joseph touched.

Beloved, let's learn quickly that without Jesus, we cannot succeed, and if we choose not to respond to His unmerited favor, He will not force it on us. God's unmerited favor is ever-flowing toward us and Jesus is waiting for us to come to the end of ourselves. He is waiting for you to stop struggling in your own attempts to somehow "deserve" His favor, and just depend on Him. So in the areas that you are still depending on your own efforts to succeed, start resting in Jesus' unmerited favor and begin experiencing His manifested presence and glory upon everything you touch!

❖

Today's Prayer

Lord Jesus, I acknowledge that without You, I cannot experience good and long-lasting success. Please increase my capacity to receive Your unmerited favor that is ever-flowing toward me. Today, I choose to depend on Your unmerited favor. I want to experience Your manifested presence and glory in everything I touch.

Today's Thought

*I will stop striving to gain what I want through my own attempts.
I am going to depend on Jesus and receive His unmerited favor.*

Today's Reflection On Favor

_____

_____

_____

_____

_____

_____

_____

_____

_____

_____

_____

_____

_____

_____

_____

_____

_____

_____

_____

What A Friend We Have In Jesus

❖

Today's Scripture

...there is a friend who sticks closer than a brother. —Proverbs 18:24

My FRIEND, GOD is with you today because of His precious Son, Jesus. For God so loved the world, He gave His only Son, and His name is Immanuel. God gave us Jesus. The presence of Jesus in your life is a free gift from God. There is no amount of good that you can do to earn the presence of Jesus. There is no number of good works that you can perform to merit His favor. His presence in your life is a free gift. Now, because you did nothing to deserve His presence in your life, there is nothing you can do that will cause His presence to leave you. Once you have received Jesus into your heart, He will never leave you nor forsake you (Hebrews 13:5)!

Jesus is a faithful, dependable and trustworthy friend.

"But Pastor Prince, when I fail, doesn't Jesus leave me?"

No, Jesus is right by your side to encourage you and restore you to wholeness. You may say, "But I don't deserve it!" That's right. That's what makes it His unmerited favor in your life. There is a beautiful psalm that says, "The steps of a good man are ordered by the Lord, and He delights in his way. Though he fall, he shall not be utterly cast down; for the Lord upholds him with His hand" (Psalm 37:23–24). When you fail, Jesus is there to uphold you. Unlike some of your so-called "friends," He does not just take off. You can count on Him. He is a faithful, dependable and trustworthy friend. Even when you have failed Him, He is right there with you, ready to pick you up and restore you to wholeness. Amen! The Bible talks about a friend who "sticks closer than a brother." That's Jesus! Beloved, lean on His constant presence. Draw on His unfailing strength and support for you today.

Today's Prayer

Lord Jesus, I thank You that even when I fall, I will not be utterly cast down because You will uphold me with Your righteous right hand. I can count on You to pick me up and restore me to wholeness. Thank You for Your faithfulness to me and for Your unfailing, dependable presence in my life every day.

Today's Thought

Even when I have failed Him, Jesus is right there with me, ready to pick me up and restore me to wholeness.

Today's Reflection On Favor

_____

_____

_____

_____

_____

_____

_____

_____

_____

_____

DAY 19

Blessed With Good Success
To Be A Blessing

❖

Today's Scripture

I will make you a great nation; I will bless you and make your name great; and you shall be a blessing. —Genesis 12:2

MAKE NO MISTAKE about this: God wants us to be successful. Yet, He does not want us to have success that will crush us. I am sure that you have heard many stories of people who receive a sudden windfall when they come into a large inheritance or strike the first prize in a lottery. However, for some of these people, the sudden wealth did not give them a better life. Instead, in many instances, we know that it corrupted and destroyed their lives.

God wants to bless you so that you can be a blessing!

Often, these people were not able to handle their so-called success, and ended up leaving their wives and allowing their families to break down before their eyes. Perhaps they bought all sorts of things and lived in huge houses. Yet, they still felt a chronic sense of loneliness, emptiness and dissatisfaction. The sad reality is that many of those who chanced upon such sudden wealth squandered it all away, and some even became bankrupt. Such results are clearly not the Jesus-kind of results, nor are they the Jesus-kind of success. Let me make it clear from the outset: God has no problem with you having money, but He does not want money to have you!

"But Pastor Prince, how can you say that God has no problem with us having money? Doesn't the Bible say that money is the root of all evil?"

51

Hold on a minute, that's not in the Bible. Let's be scripturally accurate. What the Bible says is this: "For **the love of money** is a root of all kinds of evil..." (1 Timothy 6:10). Can you see the difference? Having money does not make you evil. It is the obsession with and intense love of money that lead to all kinds of evil. Just because a person has no money in his pocket does not mean that he is holy. He may well be thinking, dreaming and lusting after money all day long. You don't need to have a lot of money to have the love of money. If a person is always purchasing lottery tickets, going to the casinos and gambling in the stock market, this person clearly has a love for money. He is obsessed with getting more money.

When God called Abraham, He said to him, "...I will bless you... and you shall be a blessing" (Genesis 12:2). We who are new covenant believers in Christ are called the seed of Abraham (Galatians 3:29) and like Abraham, we are called to be a blessing. Now, how can we be a blessing if we are not blessed in the first place? How can we be a blessing to others when we are always flat on our backs with sickness, living from hand to mouth, never having enough for our own family and always having to borrow from others? No way, my friend. God wants you healthy and strong, and He wants you to have more than enough financial resources so that you can be generous with your relatives, friends, community or anyone who needs help. How can you be in a position to help others if you need all the help you can get yourself? It's definitely not God's best for you if you barely have enough for yourself. He wants to bless you so that you can be a blessing!

❖

Today's Prayer

Father, thank You for wanting to bless me with more than enough,
so that I can be a blessing to others, especially those in need.
Give me the Jesus-kind of success that will not crush me,
but be a testimony of Your goodness and grace.

Today's Thought

God has no problem with me having money,
but He does not want money to have me!

Today's Reflection On Favor

_____

_____

_____

_____

_____

_____

_____

_____

_____

_____

_____

_____

_____

_____

_____

_____

_____

_____

_____

_____

DAY 20

The Secret To Good Success

❖

Today's Scripture

The blessing of the Lord makes one rich, and He adds no sorrow with it.
—Proverbs 10:22

GOD DOES NOT simply want you to experience success in your life. He wants you to have good success. Is there such a thing as "bad success"? Yes there is and I am sure you have seen it yourself. There are people who are high achievers according to the world's definition. Perhaps they are movers and shakers of the economy, famous celebrities who live in fabulous pads or sports stars who make millions of dollars a week hitting or kicking a ball around. However, for some of these people, what they have is only success in amassing wealth.

Having financial success alone does not equate to good success. Good success is holistic and permeates every spectrum of your life.

But, my friend, having financial success alone does not equate to good success. Good success is holistic and permeates every spectrum of your life. If you were to take a closer look at individuals who only have financial success, you would find that other areas of their lives are suffering. For instance, while they may have plenty of money, their lives could be scarred by one broken marriage after another. Beloved, being a public success but a private failure is not good success at all!

There are people who get promoted through the ranks so quickly and take on so many work responsibilities that they no longer have time to put their own kids to bed or read their little ones a bedtime story.

They become victims of their own career success, and to hang on to the "success" they have created in the cutthroat corporate world, they allow their lives to zip past them. They may have earned more money than they will ever need, but they can't enjoy their spouses and their children grow up without really knowing them.

Realize this: Even if you do win the rat race after scampering around all day, all you would have achieved is the status of number one rat! Is it really worth sacrificing your marriage and your children for that? Don't just bury yourself in climbing the corporate ladder. Make sure your ladder is placed against the right building, and don't wait till you reach the top before you realize that it's not what you really want out of life.

I often tell my congregation that they should believe God not just for a job, but also depend on His favor for a **position of influence**. However, I also remind them to be careful not to get promoted *out* of their place of blessings, because not every promotion is necessarily God's best for them.

Do you know that you can be promoted out of the good success that you are currently enjoying into a place where you enjoy only partial success? That promotion that you receive may also come with new responsibilities that will cause you to compromise your time with your family and draw you away from being in the house of God. All of a sudden, instead of being in God's house on Sunday morning and bringing your kids for a picnic after church, you find yourself in the office every weekend. Perhaps you need to respond to urgent emails, resolve major crises, attend pressing board meetings or have yet another critical business trip to go for. You see, it can all sound very legitimate, but is this the "good success" that God wants for you?

Listen carefully to what I am saying. I am all for you being promoted in your workplace. In fact, I believe that God can promote you way beyond your educational qualifications and work experience! Just look at what God did for Joseph. He was promoted from being a slave (the lowest possible position) to an overseer in Potiphar's house. And even when he was thrown into prison, the Lord's favor caused him to be promoted again and he became the overseer of all the prisoners.

Joseph experienced one promotion after another until he became the prime minister of Egypt (the highest possible position)! There is no doubt that God wants to promote and increase you. But note that Joseph's eyes were not fixed on any of the promotions that he received. His eyes were fixed on the Lord each step of the way. **That** made him safe for the next round of promotion and he grew in the **good success** that the Lord had for him.

Beloved, while you depend on His unmerited favor to bring you to a place of influence and increase, be conscious of Jesus' goodness toward you. This will keep you walking in the kind of success that truly blesses you and makes you a blessing to others.

Today's Prayer

Father, I thank You that You can and want to promote me beyond my educational qualifications, natural abilities and work experience. As You only want me to have good success, I ask that You open doors of opportunities that are good for me and shut those doors that are bad for me. Help me to always keep my eyes on Jesus so that promotions and success do not get the better of me.

Today's Thought

Fixing my eyes on Jesus makes me safe for the good success that He has for me.

Today's Reflection On Favor

_____

_____

_____

_____

DAY 21

Be Safe For Success—
Keep Your Eyes On Jesus

❖

Today's Scripture

But seek first the kingdom of God and His righteousness,
and all these things shall be added to you. —Matthew 6:33

THE WORD OF God says, "But seek first the kingdom of God and His righteousness, and all these things shall be added to you." Now, what is the kingdom of God? The apostle Paul tells us in Romans 14:17 that the kingdom of God is not eating and drinking, but "righteousness and peace and joy in the Holy Spirit."

The more you focus on beholding Jesus in all His loveliness and the less you struggle to earn things by your own merits, the more you become safe for greater success.

When you keep your eyes fixed on Jesus and pursue the kingdom of God, which is Jesus' righteousness, His peace and His joy, God's Word promises that "all these things" will be added to you. "These things" refer to what you will eat, drink and wear. Jesus tells us that you do not have to be consumed by these concerns. If your Father feeds even the birds of the air, even though they neither sow nor reap nor gather into barns, how much more will He take care of you, who are of much more value to Him than the birds (Matthew 6:25–32)!

Beloved, keep your eyes on Jesus and His finished work on the cross. He will add the things that you need in this life to you and cause you to become safe for success. Now, turn with me to the Book of Jeremiah to see what the Lord says about having riches, wisdom and might.

..."Let not a wise man boast of his wisdom, and let not the mighty man boast of his might, let not a rich man boast of his riches; but let him who boasts boast of this, that he understands and knows Me, that I am the Lord who exercises lovingkindness, justice, and righteousness on earth; for I delight in these things," declares the Lord.

—Jeremiah 9:23–24 NASB

Let us be a people who will not depend on our own wisdom, might and riches (in summary, our own merits), but rather, let our boasting (dependence) be in understanding and knowing Jesus. Know that He is gracious and full of unmerited favor toward us. Know that He executes justice against all injustices. Know that He Himself is righteousness and He clothes us with His robes of righteousness. The more you focus on beholding Jesus in all His loveliness and the less you struggle to earn things by your own merits, the more you become safe for greater success in your life.

❖

Today's Prayer

Father, make me safe for greater success. I want to know more about the loveliness of Jesus and the perfection of His love for me, so that I will learn not to depend on my wisdom and might, but to depend on Jesus and Jesus alone. Please give me a greater revelation of Jesus' righteousness, peace and joy that will help guard my heart from worry and fears and make me safe for greater success.

Today's Thought

When I go after Jesus' righteousness, peace and joy, God's Word promises that what I need in life will come after me!

Today's Reflection On Favor

_____

_____

_____

_____

_____

_____

_____

_____

_____

_____

_____

_____

_____

_____

_____

_____

_____

_____

_____

_____

DAY 22

Desire God's Unmerited Favor, Not Favoritism

Today's Scripture

And the patriarchs, becoming envious, sold Joseph into Egypt. But God was with him and delivered him out of all his troubles, and gave him favor and wisdom in the presence of Pharaoh, king of Egypt; and he made him governor over Egypt and all his house. —Acts 7:9–10

IT IS IMPORTANT for you to recognize that there is a significant difference between **God's unmerited favor** and **favoritism**. God's unmerited favor is based entirely on Jesus' merit, and we received it through His finished work at the cross. We did nothing to deserve His favor. It is completely unmerited. Favoritism, however, stinks of self-effort. Individuals who rely on favoritism for promotion have to resort to apple polishing, office politics, manipulative tactics, backstabbing and all kinds of compromises just to get what they want. They use all their efforts to open doors for themselves, and in the process, they lose themselves.

You do not have to depend on favoritism to keep opportunities open for yourself when you have God's unmerited favor!

God has a higher and better way for you. It hurts Him to see His precious children groveling like sycophants just to get ahead in life. If a door closes, so be it! Believe with full confidence that God has a better way for you. You do not have to depend on favoritism to keep opportunities open for yourself when you have God's unmerited favor!

That was how Joseph operated. He depended on the Lord for

his success, and not on favoritism, which would have required him to compromise his beliefs. When Potiphar's wife kept trying to seduce Joseph to sleep with her, Joseph stood his ground on the firm foundation of unmerited favor. By the way, I believe that Joseph faced a real temptation. Don't forget that Potiphar was a high-ranking officer. He was the captain of the guard, and a man of position, influence and wealth. As a man of the world, he would not have married an ugly woman for her inner beauty and would certainly not have married someone who looked ancient! He would definitely have chosen a young, beautiful woman to be his wife, and she was possibly one of the most beautiful women in the land.

So there is no doubt that she was a real temptation to Joseph, and that is why Joseph had to run! This woman didn't just tempt Joseph once. The Bible tells us that "she spoke to Joseph day by day," enticing him to lie with her (Genesis 39:10). But Joseph refused, saying, "There is no one greater in this house than I, nor has he [Potiphar] kept back anything from me but you, because you are his wife. How then can I do this great wickedness, and sin against **God**?" (Genesis 39:9).

From his words, it is clear that Joseph knew the source of his success, favor and blessings. He did not see giving in to Potiphar's wife as a great wickedness and sin against Potiphar alone, but against God too. He knew that every blessing that he had experienced was a result of **the Lord's** favor on him. He knew that it was not Potiphar who promoted him from the position of a lowly slave to become the overseer of Potiphar's entire estate. It was the Lord!

Similarly in your life, know and rejoice that it is the Lord who is the source of your blessings and success! You don't have to resort to trying to win the favor of significant people in your life. It is the Lord's favor on you that sets you up for recognition, promotion and increase.

Today's Prayer

Father, I thank You that You are for me and not against me. You are interested in my success and because Your unmerited favor is upon me, I do not have to resort to apple polishing, backstabbing and all kinds of compromises just to get ahead in life. Today, I rest in Your love and Your good plans to set me up for success.

Today's Thought

God alone is the source of my success, favor and blessings.

Today's Reflection On Favor

_____

_____

_____

_____

_____

_____

_____

_____

_____

_____

_____

_____

_____

_____

_____

_____

You Can Never Forfeit
The Presence Of God

❖

Today's Scripture

...For He Himself has said, "I will never leave you nor forsake you."
—Hebrews 13:5

THERE WAS A time under the law in the Old Testament where God would be with you only when you were in complete obedience. But when you failed, He would leave you. Today, however, you and I are under a completely different covenant and God will never leave us. Why? Because of what Jesus did on the cross. At the cross, He became our burnt offering. He bore our sins and carried our punishment. God's judgment against our sins fell upon Jesus, who was forsaken at the cross by His Father so that today, we can have God's constant, unceasing presence in our lives.

When you are doing right, He is with you. Even when you have failed, He is still with you!

Jesus cried out, "My God, My God, why have You forsaken Me?" so that you and I will know exactly what happened on the cross (Matthew 27:46). That is where the divine exchange took place. At the cross, Jesus took our sins and gave up the presence of God, while we took Jesus' righteousness and received the presence of God that Jesus had. God's presence is now ours for eternity. What a divine exchange!

Take a look with me at what the Bible says about our inheritance in Christ: "...For He Himself has said, 'I will never leave you nor forsake you.' So we may boldly say: 'The Lord is my helper; I will not fear. What can man do to me?'" (Hebrews 13:5–6). What confidence we can have today! Do you know what "never" here means? It means that when you are up, He is with you. When you are down, He is with you. When you are glad, He is with you. When you are sad, He is with you. When you are doing right, He is with you. Even when you have failed, He is still with you! That is what it means when Jesus said that He would **never** leave you nor forsake you!

In case you are still not convinced, let me show you what it says in the original Greek text. When God said, "I will **never** leave you **nor** forsake you," a "double negative"[1] is used to convey the strongest sense of "never" possible in the Greek language. The Greek words *ou me* are used, which in essence means, "never never" or "never ever." And this double negative appears twice in this one statement from the Lord. *Ou me* is used for both "never" and "nor." In other words, God is saying, "I will never never leave you and I will never never forsake you!" The Amplified Bible brings out the strength of what God really meant:

> I will not in any way fail you nor give you up nor leave you without support. [I will] not, [I will] not, [I will] not in any degree leave you helpless nor forsake nor let [you] down (relax My hold on you)! [Assuredly not!]
>
> —Hebrews 13:5 AMPC

Wow, that is what Jesus has done for us! He has given us the constant presence of God! My friend, settle it in your heart once and for all—God will **never** leave you! God will **never** forsake you! And if you hear anyone telling you that you can forfeit the presence of God, stop listening. Don't let that person rob you of the certainty of God's presence in your life. When God says "never ever," He means "never ever," and our God cannot lie! This means that Jesus, your prosperity, peace, provision and wisdom, is always with you. You cannot help but prosper!

❖

Father, I am so glad that I have Your constant, unceasing presence in my life because of the divine exchange at Calvary. Whether I am up or down, happy or sad, have done right or done wrong, You are with me. Your help, protection, provision, strength and shalom are on my side. I have nothing and no one to fear. Thank You!

Today's Thought

God will never ever, in any way, in any degree, leave me helpless or forsake me!

Today's Reflection On Favor

_____

_____

_____

_____

_____

_____

_____

_____

_____

_____

_____

_____

_____

_____

_____

DAY 24

Bring Jesus Into The Picture

❖

Today's Scripture

So he cried out to the Lord, and the Lord showed him a tree. When he cast it into the waters, the waters were made sweet. —Exodus 15:25

WHEN YOU STUDY your Bible knowing that the Lord is with you, you will be amazed at how God's Word comes alive. That is how I read the Word. I don't study it just to prepare for messages to preach on Sundays. I come to the Word to drink of the living waters from Jesus. I am conscious that Jesus is by my side, teaching me, speaking to my heart, and I can tell you that we have the best conversations during these times and I always come away from such times feeling refreshed and energized.

Jesus makes everything beautiful in your life.

Reading His Word has become a great personal time of intimacy between Jesus and me. I get completely lost and absorbed in His presence until I lose track of time. I can't tell you the number of times when I had looked up at my clock after digging into His Word and realized that it was already five in the morning! You know what it's like when you are enjoying a steaming cup of latte in a café with friends that you love, and you are having so much fun, laughing and sharing, that time just seems to disappear? Well, you can enjoy Jesus' presence in the same way!

Once you are conscious that Jesus is with you, reading the Bible no longer feels like a chore or duty. You won't catch yourself watching the clock going tick...tick...tick...tick...tick...and feeling as though an eternity has passed even though only five minutes has lapsed! That is what a chore feels like—as if time is standing still and you can't wait to get it over with. Bible study divorced from His presence is a dead work. But when it is like catching up with your best friend, there never seems to be enough time!

So see the Lord in the midst of everything that you do and learn to bring Him into the picture. He makes everything beautiful in your life. When you look at your past, the scars of yesterday may still be throbbing in your memories. Perhaps you were sexually abused as a child or you were emotionally hurt by someone you trusted. As you look back now, you may still feel angry, frustrated and disappointed all at the same time, and the hurt still pierces your heart. But in the midst of your pain, I want to challenge you to start involving Jesus. See the Lord holding you, gently healing your wounds. Jesus is right there restoring you, putting courage into your heart and taking away all the sense of shame and guilt.

Beloved, He wants you to know that your past will not determine the future that He has for you. Once you involve the Lord and put Him into your bitter waters, He will turn the bitterness into sweetness. That is what the Lord did for the children of Israel. When they came to a place called Marah, they could not drink its waters because they were bitter. Moses cried out to the Lord and the Lord showed him a tree, which Moses cast into the waters. When he did that, the Bible says that "the waters were made sweet."

Why did the foul-tasting, undrinkable waters become refreshing and sweet? The answer lies in the tree that was cast in. The tree is a picture of the cross on which our Lord Jesus hung, bearing every broken heart and every sting of betrayal. When you bring Jesus into your situation, He can cause every bitter experience to become sweet! Talk to Him and allow His presence to restore you to wholeness today!

Today's Prayer

Lord Jesus, I invite You to heal me of every bitter experience that I have had. Thank You for bearing every hurt and every sting of betrayal at the cross for me. I ask that You do a deep work in me to remove the hurt and pain I feel whenever I recall these bitter experiences. Please replace every negative emotion in my heart with Your love, peace and joy.

Today's Thought

My heart may have been badly broken, but Jesus is right now holding me, healing my wounds, restoring me and putting courage, peace and joy into my heart.

Today's Reflection On Favor

_____

_____

_____

_____

_____

_____

_____

_____

_____

_____

_____

_____

Practice Jesus' Presence
And 'Smell' Like Him

❖

Today's Scripture

*Then one of the servants answered and said, "Look, I have seen a son of
Jesse the Bethlehemite, who is skillful in playing, a mighty man of
valor, a man of war, prudent in speech, and a handsome person;
and the Lord is with him."* —1 Samuel 16:18

DAVID IS A wonderful example of someone who talked to the Lord and
practiced His presence all the time. Even as a young teenager taking care
of his father's sheep in the fields, he would be singing psalms and hymns
to the Lord and playing his harp.

**You cannot be in the presence of the Lord without His glory,
His majesty, His beauty, His power, His love and
His peace rubbing off on you.**

In 1 Samuel 16, the Bible records that King Saul was very unsettled,
and his servants told him that he was being troubled by a distressing
spirit. They then advised him to bring David before him to play the harp
for him, saying that evil spirits departed when David played the harp.
One of the servants gave a glowing description of David as someone
"who is skillful in playing, a mighty man of valor, a man of war, prudent
in speech, and a handsome person; and the Lord is with him." Do you
know why David could cause Saul to become refreshed just by playing
his harp? Do you know why David could have such accolades heaped
upon him? I believe that the key is in the last part of the verse: "the Lord
is with him."

A few years after Wendy and I got married, an incident happened that I will never forget. I was on my way home one day and I had stepped into a cramped elevator. A group of ladies squeezed into the same elevator as it stopped on another floor and boy, their perfumes were overpowering!

Anyway, almost dizzy from near-suffocation, I got home and kissed Wendy with my usual "Hello darling, I'm back." She looked at me and said, "That's a female fragrance. I know that fragrance." I told her, "Listen, darling, listen...honestly, just now..." And that's why it's so important to have trust in your marriage!

I am sure that you have experienced something similar before. Have you ever been in a room filled with cigarette smoke? You may not smoke, but your hair and clothes will smell of smoke even after you have left the room. In the same way, you cannot be in the presence of the Lord without His glory, His majesty, His beauty, His power, His love and His peace rubbing off on you. You begin to "smell" like Jesus, be powerful like Him and be filled with peace like Him! No wonder Acts 4:13 records this about Peter and John: "Now when they [the rulers and elders of Israel] saw the boldness of Peter and John, and perceived that they were uneducated and untrained men, they marveled. And they realized that **they had been with Jesus**." Beloved, choose to prioritize the presence of the Lord wherever you are. You will experience the undeniable evidence of His presence in your life.

❖

Today's Prayer

Lord Jesus, let it be said of me that I am a capable, wise and courageous person, not because I deserve these accolades, but because of Your constant presence with me. Every day, let Your glory, Your majesty, Your beauty, Your power, Your love and Your peace rub off more and more on me.

Becoming more like Jesus is not a matter of willpower,
but a result of spending time in His presence.

Today's Reflection On Favor

_____

_____

_____

_____

_____

_____

_____

_____

_____

_____

_____

_____

_____

_____

_____

_____

_____

_____

_____

DAY 26

The Gospel Brings
Health And Provision

❖

Today's Scripture

*If you then, being evil, know how to give good gifts to your children,
how much more will your Father who is in heaven give good
things to those who ask Him! —Matthew 7:11*

I HAVE BEEN accused of being one of those health and wealth "prosperity gospel" preachers. Actually, there is no such thing as a "prosperity gospel." There is only one gospel and that is the gospel of Jesus Christ. Through Jesus' finished work on the cross, you can depend on Him for His resurrection life to pulsate and flow in your physical body from the crown of your head to the soles of your feet. Sicknesses and diseases are not from God. On the cross, Jesus bore not just our sins, but also our sicknesses, diseases and infirmities, and "by His stripes we are healed" (Isaiah 53:5)!

**In the same way that you want your children to always
have more than enough, God wants you
to enjoy His supernatural provision.**

That's not all, my friend. On the cross, Jesus bore the curse of poverty! This is what the Word of God declares: "For you know the grace [unmerited favor] of our Lord Jesus Christ, that though He was rich, yet for your sakes He became poor, that you through His poverty might become rich" (2 Corinthians 8:9). Read 2 Corinthians 8 for yourself. The entire chapter is about money and being a blessing financially to those who are in need. So don't let anyone tell you that the verse is referring to "spiritual" riches. Let me tell you this: It is the devil who wants you sick and poor, but the God I know has paid a heavy price to redeem you from the curse of sickness and poverty!

Let's understand how God deals with us from the point of **relationship**. As a parent, how would you teach your child character and patience? With sicknesses and diseases? Of course not! There are institutions where we put such parents! Again, as a parent, how would you teach your child humility? By cursing your child with poverty for the rest of his life? No way! Now, isn't it amazing how everything becomes crystal clear when we start thinking from the point of view of a parent, and put our own children in the picture?

When you start to think along the lines of relationship, everything will converge and you will begin to see things from God's perspective. He is our Father who operates on the frequency of relationship, and through His unmerited favor in our lives, we learn character, patience and humility as we rest from our self-efforts and depend on Him. The more we know our Father, the more we become like Him. This is how God causes us to grow from glory to glory in every area of our lives. It is simply by beholding Him (2 Corinthians 3:18)!

You know that as parents, we always seek the best things for our children. How much more would our Father in heaven want the best things for us, His precious children? In the same way that you want your children to be healthy, God wants you to enjoy His divine health. And in the same way that you want your children to always have more than enough, God wants you to enjoy His supernatural provision. When He provides, get ready for a net-breaking, boat-sinking load (Luke 5:6–7). Get ready for 12 baskets full of leftovers (John 6:13)! The Bible puts things in perspective most clearly in Matthew 7:11—If you then, as imperfect parents, "know how to give good gifts to your children, how much more will your Father who is in heaven give good things to those who ask Him"!

My friend, get this right: God abhors sickness and He loathes poverty.

He gave everything He had to annihilate sickness and poverty, when He gave us His only Son, Jesus Christ, to die on the cross for us. He placed all of humanity's sin, as well as the curse of sickness and poverty on the body of Jesus. All you need to do right now is respond to Jesus' finished work—your sins have already been forgiven. Your physical body will be healed and your poverty will indeed be history!

Today's Prayer

Father, I thank You that Jesus took my sickness and poverty at the cross. I thank You that He has done all that needs to be done for me to enjoy divine health and prosperity! I ask You to take care of every one of my needs and I receive Your supernatural healing and provision for me and my loved ones today.

Today's Thought

If earthly parents who are imperfect don't want their children to be sick and poor, how much more my heavenly Father who loves me perfectly!

Today's Reflection On Favor

_____

_____

_____

_____

_____

_____

_____

_____

_____

_____

Know Your Commander In Chief

❖

Today's Scripture
Let God arise, let His enemies be scattered... —Psalm 68:1

IT IS INTERESTING to listen to how some Christians talk. You may hear them talking about what the devil did to them, how they got really mad at the devil and how they spent a whole night rebuking the devil. Such Christians may also go around town telling people what the devil has been telling them, but you don't really hear them talking about what **the Lord** has been telling them. Guess what? They are tuned in to the wrong frequency!

The best warfare to engage in is to magnify the Lord Jesus in your life.

Instead of magnifying Jesus and His presence and being conscious of Him, they are magnifying the devil and being more devil-conscious than Jesus-conscious. It's really sad! They are always talking about warfare and the devil. Do you know that the best warfare to engage in is to magnify the Lord Jesus in your life? The Bible declares, "Let God arise, let His enemies be scattered..." Amen!

Recently, I had a conversation with a medical doctor about spiritual warfare. She said to me, "When there is a condition in your body, you must know what the correct medical name for it is so that you can pray against it accurately." Then, she told me somewhat smugly, "As someone who's been in the army, you should know this: The most important military strategy is to know your enemy."

I smiled at her and said, "Actually, I believe that the most important military strategy is not to know your enemy, but to know your commander in chief and his directives for you."

My friend, do you know your commander in chief, Jesus Christ? Do you know with full assurance that His presence and unmerited favor are with you? Start practicing the presence of Jesus in your life today, and see what a difference He will bring to your situation!

Today's Prayer

Lord Jesus, I want to experience a closer walk with You. I want to know You more intimately and be conscious of Your presence and unmerited favor in my life. Help me understand Your plans and purposes for me so that I may be wise in how I spend my days.

Today's Thought

I will be Jesus-conscious, not devil-conscious.

Today's Reflection On Favor

_____

_____

_____

_____

_____

_____

_____

_____

_____

_____

DAY 28

Acknowledge Jesus' Presence
By Giving Thanks

❖

Today's Scripture

In everything give thanks; for this is the will of God in Christ Jesus for you. —1 Thessalonians 5:18

THERE ARE CHRISTIANS who know in theory that Jesus is with them, but they do not actively practice His presence. For me personally, one of the best ways to practice the presence of the Lord is to thank Him all the time. You can give thanks to Him for everything. Just say, "Lord, I thank You for this beautiful sunset. I thank You for Your love and for surrounding me with good things and good friends."

What you appreciate appreciates in value in your eyes.

There is no limit to what you can thank Him for since every good and perfect gift that we enjoy today comes directly from Him (James 1:17). Even if you have had a rough day at work and you are facing a seemingly impossible challenge, you can practice His presence. The moment you realize that your heart is heavy with worry and your mind is plagued by anxiety, share your challenge with Jesus and thank Him that this problem is not bigger than His hands. Begin to surrender it to Him and depend on Him for His strength, power and peace.

As you do that, you are already practicing the presence of the Lord. And as you honor His presence and behave like He is indeed with you, He sees it as faith in Him and intervenes on your behalf for your success in whatever situation you may be in.

It is sad when Christians behave like some husbands who bring their wives to a party, only to ignore them completely. Their wives could be right there with them physically, but these guys are so engaged with their own friends, talking about the stock market, economy or latest game on television, that their wives might as well not be with them.

Ladies, do you know men like that? Now, men who are reading this book, I know you are not like that, so don't get offended, all right? I know you cherish and love your wife. What I am trying to illustrate is that just because someone is with you physically, it does not mean that the person feels appreciated by you. Appreciation only occurs when you start acknowledging the presence of that person.

What I like to do is to look at Wendy across a room crowded with people, and when our eyes connect across the room, it is as if the rest of the people fade instantly into oblivion, and only Wendy remains. I want her to know that I appreciate her for coming along with me to that dinner event or meeting. I am not claiming that I am sensitive to Wendy all the time, but there are moments when I do want to make it a point to make her feel special. She is special to me, but to actually appreciate her and to make her feel special is something else all together. Like all husbands, I am still growing in this aspect.

Now, what does the word "appreciate" mean? It means "to increase in value." If you appreciate someone, the person increases in value in your eyes. My friend, the Lord is already with you, so start to practice His presence. Begin by thanking Him, appreciating Him and increasing His value in your eyes, and you will see Him acting on your behalf.

❖

Today's Prayer

Lord Jesus, I acknowledge Your presence and give You thanks for the many blessings that You have showered upon me. Thank You for surrounding me with good things and good friends. Thank You for the breathtaking sunrise and the birds that sang beautifully this morning. Thank You especially for always being with me in every situation and for being my wisdom, strength and success.

Today's Thought

I will give thanks to the Lord. That's how I can acknowledge His presence and appreciate Him.

Today's Reflection On Favor

_____

_____

_____

_____

_____

_____

_____

_____

_____

_____

_____

_____

_____

_____

_____

_____

_____

_____

_____

_____

_____

DAY 29

The Right Definition Of Righteousness

❖

Today's Scripture

I do not frustrate the grace of God: for if righteousness come by the law, then Christ is dead in vain. —Galatians 2:21 KJV

WHAT HAS A right understanding of your righteousness got to do with expecting good to happen to you today? Everything!

Many believers associate righteousness with a list of things that they have to do, and if they fulfill this list, they feel "righteous." Conversely, when they fail in terms of their behavior, they feel "unrighteous." But this is the wrong definition and understanding of righteousness.

We became righteous because of what Jesus did for us at the cross.

Let's go back to what the Bible has to say. Look at 2 Corinthians 5:21: "For He [God] made Him [Jesus Christ] who knew no sin to be sin for us, that we might become the righteousness of God in Him [Jesus Christ]." We are not righteous because we do right. We **became** righteous because of what **Jesus** did for us at the cross. "Righteousness," therefore, is not based on **our** right doing. It is based entirely on **Jesus'** right doing. Christianity is not about **doing right** to become righteous. It is all about **believing right** in Jesus to become righteous.

Do you realize that we have been conditioned to associate being blessed with doing right? Most belief systems are based on a system of merit whereby you need to fulfill certain requirements—give to the poor, do good to others and care for the underprivileged—to attain a certain state of righteousness. It all sounds very noble, self-sacrificial and appealing to our flesh, which likes to feel that our good works have earned us our righteousness.

But God is not looking at your nobility, sacrifices or good works to justify you. He is only interested in Jesus' humility at the cross. He looks at His Son's perfect sacrifice at Calvary to justify you and make you righteous! Attempting to be justified by your good works and trying your best to keep the Ten Commandments to become righteous is to negate the cross of Jesus Christ. It is as good as saying, "The cross is not enough to justify me. I need to depend on my good works to make myself clean and righteous before God."

The apostle Paul said, "I do not frustrate the grace [unmerited favor] of God: for if righteousness come by the law, then Christ is dead in vain." My friend, consider carefully what Paul is saying here. He is effectively saying that if you are depending on **your** good works, **your** doing and **your** ability to keep perfectly the Ten Commandments to become righteous, then Jesus died for nothing! That's what **"in vain"** means—**for nothing**! So don't frustrate the grace of God by depending on your good works to make yourself righteous and put God on your side. Jesus' sacrifice is more than enough to justify you! And when you know that you are justified, you can be confident that the unmerited favor of God is on your side and expect good to happen to you today!

❖

Today's Prayer

Father, I thank You that my being righteous is not based on what I have done or not done, but what Jesus has done at the cross. I cease from my works to be righteous and simply rest in Jesus' finished work. Help me to be established in the revelation that Jesus' sacrifice alone enables me to have Your unmerited favor on my side today.

Today's Thought

My being righteous is not based on my right doing.
It is based entirely on Jesus' right doing.

Today's Reflection On Favor

_____

_____

_____

_____

_____

_____

_____

_____

_____

_____

_____

_____

_____

_____

_____

_____

_____

_____

Righteousness Is Free For You But It Cost God Dearly

❖

Today's Scripture

But He was wounded for our transgressions, He was bruised for our iniquities; the chastisement for our peace was upon Him, and by His stripes we are healed. —Isaiah 53:5

IF YOU HAVE not watched *The Passion Of The Christ* directed by Mel Gibson, I encourage you to get the DVD and watch all that Jesus has done for you on His road to the cross. Observe the anguish that He endured in the garden of Gethsemane, where He prayed in preparation for the ordeal that He knew was to come.

Our righteousness is a result of Jesus' work and we can only receive His righteousness through His unmerited favor!

See how your King was taken by ruthless Roman soldiers, who mocked Him and rammed a crude crown fashioned from thorns onto His head. Look at how your Savior suffered lash after lash from whips designed to inflict maximum pain—whips laced with broken glass and hooks, so that every stroke ripped off flesh from His already lacerated back.

In one scene, Jesus collapsed from the blows, and I screamed in my heart, willing Him to stay down so that His tormentors would relent in their vicious assault on Him. But He did not stay down. With you and me on His mind, He clung on to the beating post and dragged Himself up to receive the full measure of the scourging, knowing that it is by His stripes that we are healed.

His agony did not end when the hardened soldiers grew tired of flogging Him. The soldiers shoved a heavy cross onto His completely bloodied back, forcing Him to carry the splintered planks toward Golgotha. After barely surviving such vicious treatment, it was no wonder that Jesus fell under the weight of the cross after staggering part of the way, and the soldiers had to force a passerby to help Him carry the cross. Our Lord was then stretched out over the cross and huge, long nails were hammered cruelly into His hands and feet.

Did Jesus endure all this for nothing? Was this all in vain?

That is precisely what Christians who insist on trying to earn their own righteousness through the law are saying.

Let me quote Paul so that you can see for yourself what I mean:

> I do not frustrate the grace [unmerited favor] of God: for if righteousness come by the law, then Christ is dead in vain.
> —Galatians 2:21 KJV

My friend, do not frustrate the grace (unmerited favor) of God in your life by looking to yourself and trying by your own efforts to make yourself righteous before God. We cannot earn God's favor and acceptance. We can only receive righteousness as a free gift from God. God's righteousness is free for us, but it cost Him dearly. He paid for it with the blood of His only begotten Son, Jesus Christ. It is a gift that can only be given freely not because it is cheap, but truly, because it is priceless!

"But Pastor Prince, how can I, who did no right, be made righteous?"

Well, answer me this first: How could Jesus, who knew no sin, become sin on the cross for us?

You see, Jesus had no sin of His own, but He took upon Himself all of humanity's sins. On the other hand, you and I had no righteousness of our own, but on that cross, Jesus took upon Himself all our sins, past, present and future, and in exchange, gave us His perfect, everlasting righteousness. Now, is this righteousness that we have received a result of our own works or **His** work? It is clear that our righteousness is a result of His work and we can only receive His righteousness through His unmerited favor!

Let me give you the clearest definition of grace (unmerited favor) in the Bible:

> And if by grace [unmerited favor], then it is no longer of works; otherwise grace [unmerited favor] is no longer grace [unmerited favor]. But if it is of works, it is no longer grace [unmerited favor]; otherwise work is no longer work.
>
> —Romans 11:6

Do you follow? There is no middle road. You are either righteous by God's unmerited favor or you are trying to merit righteousness with your own works. You are either depending on Jesus or you are depending on yourself. Because Jesus has paid so dearly for you to have His own righteousness, you can cease from your own efforts to be righteous in God's eyes to earn His favor. See yourself the righteousness of God in Christ and expect the blessings of the righteous to manifest in your life!

❖

Today's Prayer

Father, help me to always look to Jesus, who suffered a great deal for me and died for me, so that I could have His righteousness as a free gift. I fully expect all the blessings of the righteous to flood my life today.

Today's Thought

Am I depending on Jesus or am I depending on myself and my works to be righteous before God?

Today's Reflection On Favor

_____

_____

_____

_____

_____

_____

_____

_____

_____

_____

_____

_____

_____

_____

_____

_____

_____

_____

_____

_____

God Will Never Be Angry With You

❖

Today's Scripture

"For this is like the waters of Noah to Me; for as I have sworn that the waters of Noah would no longer cover the earth, so have I sworn that I would not be angry with you, nor rebuke you. For the mountains shall depart and the hills be removed, but My kindness shall not depart from you, nor shall My covenant of peace be removed," says the Lord, who has mercy on you. —Isaiah 54:9–10

A WARNING IS issued in 1 Peter 5:8—"Be sober, be vigilant; because your adversary the devil walks about **like a roaring lion**, seeking whom he may devour." I know that a lion roars to intimidate and to bring fear, but I used to wonder what kind of fear the devil tries to instill in the believer. We must **let the Bible interpret the Bible**. We can't base our interpretations on our denominational backgrounds or our experiences.

God will never be angry with us again because of what Christ has accomplished for us!

One day, I was reading Proverbs 19 when I came across verse 12: "The king's wrath is like the **roaring of a lion**, but his favor is like dew on the grass." Who is the king that this verse refers to? It is our Lord Jesus! So when the devil goes about **like a roaring lion**, he is trying to impersonate the King. He is trying to make you feel as if God is angry with you. Every time you hear preaching that leaves you with a sense that God is angry with you, guess what? You have just been roared at! But know this, beloved: God will NEVER be angry with you ever again. He only has to tell us this, but He wanted us to be so sure that He **swore** in His Word that He would never be angry with us again.

Today's verses are from Isaiah 54, which is right after the famous messianic chapter of the sufferings of Christ in Isaiah 53. Therefore, Isaiah 54 is spelling out the triumphs and spoils of His sufferings.

Do you know why God will never be angry with us again? It is because of what Christ has accomplished for us! On the cross, God poured out all His anger on the body of His Son. Jesus exhausted all the fiery indignation of a holy God against all our sins, and when all of God's judgment of our sins had been completely exhausted, He shouted, "It is finished!" (John 19:30). And because our sins have already been punished, God, who is a holy and just God, will not punish us today when we believe in what Christ has done. God's holiness is now on your side. His righteousness is now for you, not against you. You are His beloved, in whom He is well pleased because of Jesus' finished work!

The next time the devil tries to rob you of your sense of being beloved by making you think that God is angry with you, just ignore him. Ignore him when he says, "How can you call yourself a Christian?" You are a righteous, accepted and beloved child of God! When you believe this, you will have the confidence to face every challenge with boldness, knowing that you have God's unmerited favor on your side!

❖

Today's Prayer

Father, thank You for Your Word that tells me that You will never be angry with me again. Because Jesus bore the judgment of all my sins in His own body at the cross, I stand righteous before You, totally accepted, favored and loved by You. I am empowered by Your perfect love to reign over my circumstances today!

Today's Thought

*Because of what Jesus has accomplished at the cross for me,
God's righteousness is for me, not against me!*

Today's Reflection On Favor

_____

_____

_____

_____

_____

_____

_____

_____

_____

_____

_____

_____

_____

_____

_____

_____

_____

_____

_____

_____

DAY 32

What's Your Response To The Voice Of Accusation?

❖

Today's Scripture

In righteousness you shall be established; you shall be far from oppression,
for you shall not fear; and from terror, for it shall not come near you.
—Isaiah 54:14

IT IS IMPORTANT for you to be established in the righteousness of Christ, because it will determine how you respond to the voice of accusation when you are believing God for big things, and trusting Him for answered prayers.

Right believing always leads to right living.

"Who do you think you are?"

"Don't you remember how you yelled at your spouse this morning? Why should God give you favor for your important presentation at the office today?"

"Look at how easily you lose your cool on the road. How can you have the cheek to expect good things to happen to you?"

"You call yourself a Christian? When was the last time you read your Bible? What have you done for God? Why should God heal your child?"

Do these accusations sound awfully familiar? Now, how you respond to this voice of accusation will expose what you really believe. This is the litmus test of what you believe. This is where the rubber meets the road! A person could think, "Yeah, you are right. I don't deserve this. How can I expect God's favor to be on me for my presentation at the office when I was so harsh with my wife this morning?" Now, that's the response of someone who believes that he needs to earn his own righteousness and place of acceptance before God. This person believes that he can expect good from God only when his conduct is good and his own checklist of self-imposed requirements are met to the hilt.

He would probably storm into his office, still seething with anger at his wife. Worst of all, he feels cut off from the presence of Jesus because of his anger and thinks that he does not qualify to ask for God's favor for his presentation. He steps into the boardroom disheveled and disorganized. He forgets his points and fumbles, causing his company to lose that major account. His bosses are disappointed with him and give him a huge tongue-lashing. Frustrated and shamed, he drives home like a maniac, sounding his horn at every car that does not move the instant the traffic lights turn green. When he gets home, he is even more upset with his wife because he blames her for putting him in a foul mood in the morning, for his terrible presentation and for the loss of the major account! It's all HER fault!

Now, see the difference if this person thinks, "Yeah, you are right. I don't deserve to have God's favor at all because I lost my temper with my wife this morning. But you know what? I am not looking at what I deserve. I am looking at what Jesus deserves. Even right now, Jesus, I thank You that You see me perfectly righteous. Because of the cross and Your perfect sacrifice, I can expect God's unmerited favor at my presentation. Every one of my shortcomings, even the tone I used this morning, is covered by Your righteousness. I can expect good not because I am good, but because You are good! Amen!"

See the amazing difference? This person is established upon Jesus' righteousness and not his own right doing or good behavior. He goes to work depending on the unmerited favor of Jesus, and he aces the presentation and clinches a major account for his company. His bosses are impressed by his performance and mark him for the next round of promotion. He drives home with peace and joy, feeling the Father's love and favor. Consequently, he is more patient with other drivers.

Now, does this mean that he sweeps all his failings under the carpet and pretends that they never happened? No way! This man, full of the consciousness that the Lord is with him, will find the strength in Christ to apologize to his wife for the tone he had used on her. You see, a heart that has been touched by unmerited favor cannot hold on to unforgiveness, anger and bitterness. Which of the above accounts demonstrate true holiness? Of course, it is the second account. Depending on God's favor results in a life of practical holiness. Right believing always leads to right living!

Today's Prayer

Father, establish me in the righteousness of Christ, so that I may respond with grace when the rubber meets the road. Even when I know that I have failed, I choose to see myself as You do—in Jesus' righteousness, and I expect Your unmerited favor to work for me despite my failures. Thank You for the gift of righteousness, which causes me to reign over everything in my life.

Today's Thought

Depending on and experiencing God's favor leads to practical holiness.

Today's Reflection On Favor

_____

_____

_____

_____

_____

_____

_____

_____

Grace When You Least Deserve It

❖

Today's Scripture

...not having my own righteousness, which is from the law, but that which is through faith in Christ, the righteousness which is from God by faith. —Philippians 3:9

THE GRACE OF God is the unearned, undeserved and unmerited favor of God. When God answers you in your most undeserving moment, **that** is grace. **That** is His amazing, unmerited favor! At your lowest point, in your darkest hour, His light shines through for you and you become a recipient of His unmerited favor, and a recipient of favor can't help but want to extend grace to others.

The more righteousness-conscious you are, the more you will experience God's unmerited favor.

My friend, in and of ourselves, we don't deserve anything good. But because we are in Christ and in His righteousness, God will not withhold any blessing from our lives today. Our part is not to struggle in our own works and be independent from God, but to focus on receiving all that we need from Him.

I believe that the more righteousness-conscious you are, the more you will experience God's unmerited favor. When the voice of disqualification comes to remind you of all the areas that you have fallen short in, **that's** the time to turn to Jesus who qualifies you and hear His voice. That is the true fight of faith! The fight of faith is to fight to believe that you are made righteous by faith and not by works. Paul, speaking of his own achievements under the law, said that he counts them all "as rubbish, that I may gain Christ and be found in Him, not having **my own righteousness, which is from the law**, but that which is through faith in Christ, **the righteousness which is from God by faith**" (Philippians 3:8–9).

So there are clearly two types of righteousness in the Bible: (1) A righteousness that comes from your obedience and from you trying to earn your way to attain it. (2) A righteousness that comes from faith in Jesus Christ.

Only one of these has a solid, unshakable foundation. One is built upon **you** and **your** ability to keep the law, while the other is built upon the Rock of all ages—Jesus Christ. One can only give you the occasional confidence to ask for God's favor, depending on how well you perceive you have done. The other gives you confidence ALL THE TIME to access His unmerited favor, even when you feel that you are greatly undeserving.

What do you want to depend on when push comes to shove—your wavering righteousness or the perfect, rock-solid righteousness of Jesus? It is your faith in the righteousness of Jesus that gives you the right to God's unmerited favor. Today, because of what Jesus did on the cross, you can expect good things to happen to you. You can ask God for big things and reach out to the blessed destiny that He has for you and your family. His righteousness is your right to God's unmerited favor! Don't let any voice of accusation tell you otherwise!

❖

Today's Prayer

Father, I thank You that at my lowest point, in my darkest hour, the light of Your favor still shines through to me. I thank You that I can experience good things from You even when I am most undeserving, because it's not about my obedience, but the perfect obedience of Your Son Jesus at the cross.

Today's Thought

I have access to God's favor all the time,
even when I feel most undeserving!

Today's Reflection On Favor

_____

_____

_____

_____

_____

_____

_____

_____

_____

_____

_____

_____

_____

_____

_____

_____

_____

_____

_____

_____

DAY 34

You Have God's Presence And Favor Regardless Of Your Circumstances

❖

Today's Scripture

Where can I go from Your Spirit? Or where can I flee from Your presence? If I ascend into heaven, You are there; if I make my bed in hell, behold, You are there. If I take the wings of the morning, and dwell in the uttermost parts of the sea, even there Your hand shall lead me, and Your right hand shall hold me. —Psalm 139:7–10

HEBREWS 13:5 SAYS that God's presence in your life is a guaranteed constant. But I want you to know that you cannot evaluate God's presence and His unmerited favor in your life based on your circumstances. To help you understand what this means, let's look at the life of Joseph.

Joseph considered not his circumstances, but kept his focus on the presence of the Lord.

Joseph refused the advances made by Potiphar's wife, and as the common saying goes, "Hell hath no fury like a woman scorned"! She maliciously accused Joseph of attempting to rape her, brandishing as "evidence" the garments that Joseph had left in her hands when he fled from her. When Potiphar heard his wife telling her version of the story, his anger was aroused and he seized Joseph, stripped him from the place of authority he had given him and threw him into prison.

Just put yourself in Joseph's shoes. What is happening here? It sounds all too familiar, doesn't it? With the painful memory of his brothers casting him into the pit still fresh in his mind, here he is once again, cast into a dungeon even though he was innocent. Any average person would be bitter and angry with God! Most people would ask, "Where is God? Why had God brought him this far, only to abandon and forsake him? How could this happen? Where is the justice against this false accusation?"

But Joseph was literally no "average Joe"! He knew that the Lord would never leave him nor forsake him. Joseph considered not his circumstances, but kept his focus on the presence of the Lord. Regardless of whether he was a common slave, an overseer in Potiphar's house or now a prisoner facing the prospect of life imprisonment for a crime he did not even commit, Joseph did not evaluate God's unmerited favor in his life based on his circumstances. Instead of getting bitter, he kept his hope in the Lord. Instead of throwing in the towel and giving up on God and on life, he kept his confidence, knowing that all his success was wrapped up in the presence of the Lord.

And boy, did the Lord deliver him! I want you to read this for yourself to see what the Lord did for Joseph:

> But the Lord was with Joseph and showed him mercy, and He gave him favor in the sight of the keeper of the prison. And the keeper of the prison committed to Joseph's hand all the prisoners who were in the prison; whatever they did there, it was his doing. The keeper of the prison did not look into anything that was under Joseph's authority, because the Lord was with him; and whatever he did, the Lord made it prosper.
>
> —Genesis 39:21–23

What does this tell you? If you refuse to bow to your circumstances and continue to be conscious of the Lord's presence, wherever you are placed, whatever your environment, you will rise to prominence. You will have favor with your bosses and they will promote you to man-in-charge. And whatever you do will prosper!

Today's Prayer

*Father, keep me mindful of Your loving presence wherever I am.
And because You are with me and for me, I thank You that
I will have favor with people and I will prosper in all that I do!*

Today's Thought

*God's presence in my life will cause me to prosper
regardless of the location or position I am in.*

Today's Reflection On Favor

_____

_____

_____

_____

_____

_____

_____

_____

_____

_____

_____

_____

_____

_____

_____

_____

_____

With God's Favor, You Can't Help But Prosper

❖

Today's Scripture

...though a righteous man falls seven times, he rises again...
—Proverbs 24:16 NIV

WHEN THE UNMERITED favor of God is upon you wherever you are, like it was upon Joseph, (1) you cannot help but find favor, (2) everything that you do cannot help but prosper, and (3) you cannot help but experience increase and promotion beyond your wildest imagination!

Your lowest points are launching pads to God's greatest promotions.

Can you see that this was the consistent pattern in Joseph's life? It didn't matter if he was a slave or prisoner. The same applies to you. When the unmerited favor of God is upon you, you are like a rubber ball in a pool of water. Natural circumstances can try to push you down and keep you suppressed under water, but the unmerited favor of God will always cause you to POP right up to the top!

Don't be discouraged by your current circumstances. I know things may sometimes appear bleak, dismal and perhaps even devastating, but it ain't over, my friend. I wrote this book to tell you that it ain't over! I don't believe for one moment that among the millions of books in publication right now, you are holding this particular one by chance or coincidence. This is a divine appointment and I believe that God is saying this to you: "Don't give up. It ain't over!"

There are many times where the lowest points in your life are actually launching pads to God's greatest promotion in your life. It was so for Joseph! Let's rewind the tape and observe the fingerprints of the Lord through the ups and downs of Joseph's life. If Joseph had not been betrayed by his brothers, he would not have been sold as a slave. If he had not been sold as a slave, he would not have been in Potiphar's house. If he was not in Potiphar's house, he would not have been thrown into an Egyptian prison meant specifically for the king's prisoners. If he was not in that specific prison, he would not have interpreted the dreams of Pharaoh's officers. If he had not interpreted their dreams, he would not have been summoned to interpret Pharaoh's dream two years later. If he had not interpreted Pharaoh's dream, Pharaoh would not have promoted Joseph to become his prime minister over the entire Egyptian empire!

This is what Pharaoh said to Joseph: "Inasmuch as God has shown you all this, there is no one as discerning and wise as you. You shall be over my house, and all my people shall be ruled according to your word; only in regard to the throne will I be greater than you...See, I have set you over all the land of Egypt" (Genesis 41:39–41). When we look back, it is clear that the Lord had turned Joseph's darkest hour into his finest hour!

God's presence with Joseph and His unmerited favor caused Joseph to be promoted from the pit to the palace, from the dunghill to Capitol Hill, from the outhouse to the White House. Stop looking at your circumstances and stop allowing them to discourage you. The same Lord who was with Joseph is with you right now. You cannot fail! You can expect to see success beyond your present circumstances!

❖

Today's Prayer

Father, I thank You that it's not all over for me. I may be at a low point now, but because of Your presence and favor in my life, You will pull me out of the pit and place me on high ground. I cannot help but experience increase and promotion beyond my wildest dreams because You are with me!

Today's Thought

The same Lord who was with Joseph is with me right now.
And like Joseph, I will experience increase and
promotion regardless of my circumstances!

Today's Reflection On Favor

_____

_____

_____

_____

_____

_____

_____

_____

_____

_____

_____

_____

_____

_____

_____

_____

_____

_____

_____

_____

DAY 36

Your Right To God's Unmerited Favor

❖

Today's Scripture

For He [God] made Him [Jesus Christ] who knew no sin to be sin for us, that we might become the righteousness of God in Him [Jesus Christ]. —2 Corinthians 5:21

THERE IS NO doubt that all believers want to experience God's unmerited favor in their lives. All of us want to experience success in our marriages, families, careers as well as ministries. We all want to enjoy God's best and richest blessings. We want His provision, health and power flowing mightily in our lives, and we know that all these blessings are wrapped up in God's unmerited favor. When His unmerited favor is on your side, nothing can stand against you. But if His favor is unmerited, how can we qualify for it? If we cannot earn, deserve or merit it, how can we be confident that we have His unmerited favor?

Your righteousness in Christ is the sure foundation on which you can build your expectations to receive God's unmerited favor.

One of the key things that I desire to do in this book is to build upon the existing teachings on favor and to give believers a firm foundation on **why they have the right to God's unmerited favor** in their lives today. Do you know the answers to the following questions?

Why can you expect good to happen to you?

Why can you enjoy God's unmerited favor?

Why can you ask God for big things?

Beloved, your answers are all found on the Mount of Golgotha, the place of the skull. It's the place where the sinless Man became sin, so that you and I can become the righteousness of God in Him. His righteousness is **your right** to God's unmerited favor.

You can expect good...

You can enjoy God's unmerited favor...

You can ask God for big things...

...because you have been made the righteousness of God through Jesus' sacrifice on the cross!

Don't just take my word for it. Look at 2 Corinthians 5:21 again: "For He [God] made Him [Jesus Christ] who knew no sin to be sin for us, that we might become the righteousness of God in Him [Jesus Christ]."

Your righteousness in Christ is the sure foundation on which you can build your expectations to receive God's unmerited favor. God sees you through the lens of the cross of His Son, and as Jesus is today deserving of blessings, peace, health and favor, so are you (1 John 4:17)!

❖

Today's Prayer

Father, I thank You that Jesus has paid the price for me to have Your unmerited favor. He took my sins and gave me His righteousness. And because I am righteous in Christ, I expect blessings such as peace and health to crown my head. I rest on Your Word that declares that as Jesus is, so am I in this world.

Today's Thought

God gives me what Jesus deserves because I am
the righteousness of God in Christ.

Today's Reflection On Favor

You Are Under The New Covenant Of Unmerited Favor

❖

Today's Scripture

By calling this covenant "new," He has made the first one obsolete; and what is obsolete and aging will soon disappear. —Hebrews 8:13 NIV

YOU ARE UNDER the new covenant of unmerited favor through Jesus' finished work. The old covenant based on your works is now obsolete. Look at what the New International Version of Hebrews 8:13 says: "By calling this covenant 'new,' he has made the first one obsolete; and what is obsolete and aging will soon disappear."

Under the law, even the best failed. Under grace, even the worst can be saved!

Read this verse in your Bible carefully. It is not Joseph Prince who said that the old covenant is obsolete. I am just reiterating what I read in my Bible. God's Word tells us in no uncertain terms that the covenant of Moses is antiquated and obsolete. It is no longer relevant for the new covenant believer who is in Christ today! So it is not me who found fault with the old covenant of the law. **God Himself** found fault with the old covenant of law.

Let's look at another verse:

> For if that first covenant had been faultless, then no place would have been sought for a second.
>
> —Hebrews 8:7

The Living Bible captures the apostle Paul's exasperation with the old covenant of law: "The old agreement didn't even work. If it had, there would have been no need for another to replace it. But God himself found fault with the old one..." (Hebrews 8:7–8 TLB).

Think about this objectively for a moment. Just for a second, put aside all the traditional teachings that you have heard or read. Let's reason together, not based on what man says, but based completely on what God has said in His Word. His Word is our only unshakable premise. Based on this portion of the Scripture that we have just read together, if there was nothing wrong with the old covenant of law, why would God give up His one and only precious Son to be brutally crucified on the cross, so that He could cut a new covenant with us? Why would He be willing to pay such a heavy price, allowing Jesus to be publicly humiliated, and to suffer inhumane violence, if there wasn't something fundamentally wrong with the old covenant of law?

The cross demonstrated that God found fault with the old covenant and was determined to make it obsolete. He was determined to rescue us from our sins by cutting a new covenant with His Son Jesus. That's the amazing unconditional love that God has for you and me. He knew that no man could be justified and made righteous by the law. Only the blood of His Son would be able to justify us and make us righteous in Christ.

In all of Israel's 1,500 years under the covenant of law, not a single person was made righteous by the law. Even the best of them, such as David, failed. The Bible describes him as a man after God's own heart (1 Samuel 13:14, Acts 13:22). But even he failed—he committed adultery with Bathsheba and had her husband Uriah killed. What hope then do you and I have under the law?

Thank God that under the new covenant of His unmerited favor, even the worst of us can call upon the name of Jesus and receive Him as our personal Lord and Savior. In an instant, we can be made righteous by faith in Jesus' mighty name! Under the law, even the best failed. Under grace, even the worst can be saved!

What does all this mean for us? It means that we no longer have to depend on our own works to earn God's blessings, approval and favor. Today, my friend, we can depend on His unmerited favor for our peace, wholeness and success through Jesus Christ's perfect sacrifice.

Today's Prayer

Father, I thank You that I am not under the old covenant of law today, where even the best of us will fail, but I'm under the new covenant of Your unmerited favor. Thank You for putting me under this new covenant where I don't have to work to earn Your blessings and favor. Instead, I can simply rest, knowing that I have Your blessings, approval and favor because Jesus secured them for me by His sacrifice at the cross. Today, I rest in Your unmerited favor for every success.

Today's Thought

The law condemns me at my best. Grace saves me at my worst and gives me God's unmerited favor for my peace, wholeness and success.

Today's Reflection On Favor

_____

_____

_____

_____

_____

_____

_____

_____

_____

_____

_____

DAY 38

Know Your Covenant Rights In Christ

❖

Today's Scripture
My people are destroyed for lack of knowledge... —Hosea 4:6

I CANNOT EMPHASIZE enough how vitally important it is for a believer today to know that he is under the new covenant of God's unmerited favor and no longer under the law. Many good, well-meaning and sincere believers today are defeated by their lack of knowledge of the new covenant and all the benefits that Jesus has purchased for them at the cross.

What we need is a greater revelation and appreciation of Jesus and everything that He has done for us!

"But Pastor Prince, we should not be looking at benefits when we believe in Jesus."

I am glad that you brought up this point. Let's look at what the psalmist thinks about this: "Bless the Lord, O my soul; and all that is within me, bless His holy name! Bless the Lord, O my soul, and **forget not all His benefits**: Who forgives all your iniquities, who heals all your diseases, who redeems your life from destruction, who crowns you with lovingkindness and tender mercies, who satisfies your mouth with good things, so that your youth is renewed like the eagle's." (Psalm 103:1–5)

Beloved, this is the heart of God. He wants you to remember **all** the benefits that Jesus has purchased for you with His blood! It is His heart to see you enjoying every single benefit, every single blessing and every single favor from Him in the new covenant of His grace. Forgiveness of sin is yours. Health is yours. Divine protection is yours. Favor is yours. Good things and the renewal of youth are yours! These are all precious gifts from the Lord to you, and it brings Him unspeakable joy when He sees you enjoying these gifts and succeeding in life. But it is the **lack of knowledge** of what Jesus has accomplished at the cross that has robbed many believers of enjoying these good gifts and benefits.

This reminds me of a story I read of a man who visited an impoverished old lady who was dying. As he sat next to her bed in the cramped confines of her dilapidated home, a single frame hanging on her spartan wall caught his attention.

Instead of a picture, the frame held a yellowed piece of paper with some writing on it. He asked the lady about that piece of paper and she replied, "Well, I can't read, so I don't know what it says. But a long time ago, I used to work for a very wealthy man who had no family. Just before he died, he gave me this piece of paper and I've kept it in remembrance of him for the past 40 or 50 years now." The man took a closer look at the framed contents, hesitated for a moment, then said, "Do you know that this is actually the will and testament of that man? It names you as the sole beneficiary of all his wealth and property!"

For close to 50 years, that lady had lived in abject poverty, working day and night to eke out a meager existence for herself. During all this time, she was actually the owner of a sprawling estate and enviable riches. However, her own ignorance had utterly robbed her of a life of wealth and luxury that she could have enjoyed. It is a sad story, but what is even sadder is that this tragedy is played out every day in the lives of believers who do not realize the inheritance that Jesus bequeathed them when He gave up His life at the cross.

What we need today are not more laws to govern believers. What we need is a greater revelation and appreciation of Jesus and everything that He has done for us! In Hosea 4:6, God lamented, "My people are destroyed for lack of knowledge..." Let's not be numbered among these people. Instead, let us be a people who are full of the knowledge of

Jesus, His person, His love and His finished work. Don't allow your ignorance to rob you any more. Find out all about your covenant rights in Christ today!

Today's Prayer
Father, I thank You that You forgive all my iniquities and heal all my diseases. Thank You for redeeming my life from destruction, crowning me with lovingkindness and tender mercies, and satisfying my mouth with good things, so that my youth is renewed like the eagle's. Help me remember all these benefits every day, and show me more of Jesus, His finished work and my covenant rights in Him.

Today's Thought
I will bless the Lord and forget not all His benefits.

Today's Reflection On Favor

_____

_____

_____

_____

_____

_____

_____

_____

_____

_____

_____

_____

_____

What The New Covenant Hinges On

❖

Today's Scripture

For I will be merciful to their unrighteousness, and their sins and their lawless deeds I will remember no more. —Hebrews 8:12

TODAY, BECAUSE OF the cross, you are under the new covenant of grace. Now, what does the new covenant hinge on? Beloved, God is so good. The new covenant that God has made is not dependent on anything that you and I must do because He knows that we will always fail. Listen carefully. The new covenant works because of one thing only, and it is the last clause of the new covenant—"**For** I will be merciful to their unrighteousness, and their sins and their lawless deeds I will remember no more." To the measure that you have a revelation of this clause and all its blessings, to that measure you will walk in it.

The new covenant works *because* God says that He will be merciful to our unrighteousness, and our sins and lawless deeds He will remember no more!

Note the word "For." It means "because." The new covenant works **because** God says that He will be merciful to our unrighteousness, and our sins and lawless deeds He will remember no more! "No more" means that there was a time God remembered our sins, even to punish them to the third and fourth generations (Exodus 20:5). This is found in the Ten Commandments. However, today, God says emphatically, "No more!" (It is the double negative that is used in the Greek.) "No more" means that God will never again remember our sins against us because He remembered (to punish) all our sins in the body of His Son. Jesus bore God's punishment of our sins on the cross. Now, we can walk in the new covenant and hear God say, "Your sins and lawless deeds I remember no more."

My friend, the new covenant works because of the last clause. In other words, because of Hebrews 8:12, God can put His laws in our minds and write them on our hearts, and all of us can know Him and be led by Him. It is His mercy toward us that enables us to hear Him and be led by Him to victory in every situation!

Today's Prayer

Father, I thank You that the new covenant is all about You doing for me what I cannot do for myself. And I am so glad that the benefits and privileges of the new covenant are mine because my sins and lawless deeds You remember no more! Today, I can be led by You and know You intimately all because You will by no means record my sins or hold them against me.

Today's Thought

Because of Jesus' sacrifice, God does not remember my sins and He has given me all the benefits of the new covenant!

Today's Reflection On Favor

_____

_____

_____

_____

_____

_____

_____

_____

_____

It's Written On Your Heart

❖

Today's Scripture

For it is God who works in you both to will and to
do for His good pleasure. —Philippians 2:13

GOD HAS MADE it so easy for us in the new covenant to be directed by His wisdom and love. We no longer have to run to prophets to find out His will for us. He Himself leads us! For those of you who want to serve the Lord, but don't know where to start, just ask yourself what is in your heart. If you have a desire to work among children, then do so. As a new covenant believer, that's how your Father leads you. He puts His laws in your mind and writes them on your heart!

God speaks to you directly and He has made it easy for you to know His will through His promptings in your heart.

Perhaps you feel a prompting to bless someone financially, even though the person looks prosperous. Follow that prompting because today, God speaks to you directly and He has made it easy for you to know His will through His promptings in your heart. We all know how looks can be deceiving. For example, many con artists believe that church folks are gullible. Therefore, they dress down with a well-rehearsed sob story so as to move you to give to them. On the other hand, there are noble people who dress up on Sundays to honor the occasion, but they may be in dire straits financially. Hence, we need to follow the promptings of our hearts and not the sight of our eyes. So when you feel a desire to do something good for someone, do it, knowing that you have a brand-new heart that hears God, and that it is God who works in you both the willingness and the ability to do it!

❖

Today's Prayer

Father, I thank You that You simply write Your will for me on my heart. And I thank You that You not only give me the desire or willingness to do what You want me to do, but You also give me the strength and ability to do it! Thank You for leading me from the inside in all that I need to do today.

Today's Thought

God puts His desires in my heart and it is He who empowers me to do them.

Today's Reflection On Favor

_____

_____

_____

_____

_____

_____

_____

_____

_____

_____

_____

_____

_____

_____

Practice Jesus' Presence
In Your Career

❖

Today's Scripture

For You, O Lord, will bless the righteous; with favor You will surround him as with a shield. —Psalm 5:12

WHEREVER YOU ARE, whatever it is that you do, with the Lord's presence and His unmerited favor covering you, there is no way you will not be a success. When I started working in my early twenties, I kept on practicing the presence of Jesus and in a short time, became the top salesperson in my company. I not only closed the biggest deals for my company, but I also secured the greatest frequency of sales transactions.

**Whatever vocation you are in, you can experience
the presence of Jesus and His unmerited favor,
and He will make you a success!**

I started as one of the lowest-paid employees in the company, but the Lord consistently promoted me, and gave me different income streams from within the same company until I became one of the highest-paid employees in that organization. Please understand that I am not sharing this with you to put a feather in my cap. I know beyond the shadow of a doubt that all the successes that I have experienced in my professional career are a result of Jesus' presence and unmerited favor in my life.

I shared with you about my professional career (before I entered full-time ministry) so that you will not walk away thinking that I have personally experienced good success from the Lord only because I am a pastor. No. Like I mentioned earlier, whatever vocation you are in, you can experience the presence of Jesus and His unmerited favor, and **He** will make you a success!

Whether you are a chef, driver or consultant, it doesn't matter. God is on your side to bless and make you a success. Of course, you understand that I am referring to only morally upright professions. You cannot depend on God's unmerited favor if you are in an industry that requires you to compromise on your Christian morals. If you are involved in a morally corrupt industry or a job that expects you to lie, cheat or deceive, my advice to you is to get out! You do not have to depend on a job that puts you in a morally compromising position for your income. God loves you intimately and He has something so much better in store for you. Trust Him.

God is here to save you from destroying yourself. He wants to give you good success and He loves you too much to see you remain in a job that forces you to compromise. The Bible says, "A good name is to be chosen rather than great riches, loving favor rather than silver and gold" (Proverbs 22:1). God has a higher way and better plan for your life. You can walk in it today by depending on His unmerited favor to provide for and prosper you!

❖

Today's Prayer

Father, I thank You that Your presence and unmerited favor are all that I need to enjoy good success in my career. Thank You for always being on my side and for giving me Your supernatural success in my career and relationships.

The presence of Jesus and His unmerited favor
will propel me forward in my career!

Today's Reflection On Favor

_____

_____

_____

_____

_____

_____

_____

_____

_____

_____

_____

_____

_____

_____

_____

_____

_____

_____

_____

_____

_____

DAY 42

Perfect Sacrifice, Complete Forgiveness

❖

Today's Scripture

And you, being dead in your trespasses and the uncircumcision of your flesh, He has made alive together with Him, having forgiven you all trespasses. —Colossians 2:13

You WILL NEVER be sure that you have God's unmerited favor if you are not sure if God has forgiven you of your sins. Beloved, I want you to know that your sins are forgiven not according to the riches of your good works, but according to the riches of God's grace (unmerited favor). All your sins—past, present and future—have been forgiven. Don't draw a timeline of God's forgiveness of your sins. There are some Christians who believe that the forgiveness they received spans only from the day they were born to the day they became Christians. From that point onwards, they think that they need to tread very carefully in case they lose their salvation. This belief is simply unscriptural. Colossians 2:13 states clearly that we have been forgiven of **all** our sins.

On the cross, Jesus took upon Himself all the sins that you will commit in your lifetime, and once for all paid the full price for all your sins.

Does "all" mean the same thing to you as it does to me? My Bible says that all our sins have been forgiven by Jesus' one sacrifice on the cross. We have been forgiven once and for all! The high priests in the old covenant had to offer sacrifices for sins daily. But Jesus, our perfect new covenant High Priest, offered the complete, perfect sacrifice **"once for all** when He offered up Himself" (Hebrews 7:27). On the cross, He took upon Himself all the sins that you will commit in your lifetime, and once for all paid the full price for all your sins. Christ does not need to be crucified again for your future sins. In fact, all your sins were in the future when He died on the cross. So when you received Jesus into your heart, ALL your sins were completely forgiven!

Now that you know that your sin debt has been completely cleared and settled by Jesus on your behalf, don't expect God to deal with you according to your sins. When something negative happens, don't imagine that God is coming after you because of what you did in the past. Instead, take God at His Word and expect to enjoy the benefits of the heavy price Jesus paid at the cross for you. We sowed nothing good, but through Jesus, we have reaped every good blessing. That, my friend, is called unmerited favor. And you honor what He has done for you by thanking Him and expecting these blessings to manifest in your life every day.

❖

Today's Prayer

Father, Your word is true: ALL the sins that I have and will ever commit have been forgiven by You because of Jesus. He took every one of my sins at the cross and was punished to the full. Therefore, I know that I am righteously and justly forgiven. My forgiveness is based on the sure and perfect sacrifice of Jesus. Thank You for extending such unmerited favor to me!

Today's Thought

ALL is forgiven because of Jesus' perfect sacrifice.

Today's Reflection On Favor

_____

_____

_____

_____

DAY 43

God Is Satisfied With You

❖

Today's Scripture
...He made us accepted in the Beloved. —Ephesians 1:6

W HEN I WAS a teenager, I used to belong to a Christian fellowship group. We would sing this song which you may be familiar with. It went like this: "Is He satisfied, is He satisfied, is He satisfied with me? Have I done my best? Have I stood the test? Is He satisfied with me?"[1] Let me just say that 10 out of 10 times when we sang this song, I would always believe that God was **not** satisfied with me. When we look to ourselves, all there is to see is the inadequacy and futility of our ability and performance. In and of ourselves, we will never meet God's standard for Him to be satisfied with us. We will always fall short!

God will not punish the believer again, not because He has gone soft on sin, but because all our sins have already been punished in the body of Jesus.

You can imagine how condemned we felt each time we sang this song. After all, we had never been taught that God was satisfied with His Son's sacrifice at the cross, and we did not understand what the new covenant of grace was all about. We were young and zealous for God, but defeated by our lack of knowledge.

With all due respect to the songwriter, whom I believe had the best intentions when he wrote the song, this song is not based on the new covenant of God's unmerited favor. It negates the cross and places the emphasis back on you—what **you** must do, what **you** must perform and what **you** must achieve for God to be satisfied with you. But the question to ask today is not if God is satisfied with you. The question that we need to ask is this: Is God satisfied with the cross of Jesus? And the answer is this: He is completely satisfied!

At the cross, our acceptance is found. There, Jesus cried out with His last breath, "It is finished!" (John 19:30) The work is complete. The full punishment for all our sins was exacted on Jesus at the cross. God will not punish the believer again, not because He has gone soft on sin, but because all our sins **have already been punished** in the body of Jesus. God's holiness and His justice are now on your side! Today, God is not assessing you based on what you have or have not done. He is assessing you based on what Jesus has done. Is God satisfied with Jesus today? Yes, of course He is! Then, to the same extent that God is satisfied with Jesus, He is satisfied with you.

God's own Son had to be crushed at Calvary for this blessing to become a reality in your life. The gift of His unmerited favor and His righteousness is only a free gift for you today because the full payment for this gift was exacted upon Jesus' body. The cross made all the difference! Don't let anyone hoodwink you into thinking that you need to pay for your own sins. Don't let anyone deceive you with the lie that your eternal salvation in Christ is uncertain and shakable!

❖

Today's Prayer

Father, I thank You that Your holiness and justice are now on my side because of Jesus' sacrifice for me. I thank You that You are not assessing me based on what I have or have not done, but You are assessing me based on what Jesus has done. And because You are fully satisfied with Jesus, You are fully satisfied with me today!

Today's Thought

To the same extent that God is satisfied with Jesus,
He is satisfied with me.

Today's Reflection On Favor

You Have Been Forgiven Much

❖

Today's Scripture

Therefore I say to you, her sins, which are many, are forgiven, for she loved much. But to whom little is forgiven, the same loves little.
—*Luke 7:47*

LET'S LOOK AT Luke 7:36–50 to see what Jesus said about the forgiveness of sins. Simon, a Pharisee, had invited Jesus to his house. While Jesus was seated at the table in Simon's house, a woman came to Him. She began to weep and she washed His feet with her tears. Then, she wiped His feet with her hair, kissed them and anointed them with fragrant oil.

You will only love Jesus much when you experience His lavish grace and unmerited favor in forgiving you of all your sins—past, present and future.

When Simon saw this, he said to himself, "This Man, if He were a prophet, would know who and what manner of woman this is who is touching Him, for she is a sinner." Even though Simon did not speak aloud, it is interesting that Jesus answered him by posing this question to him: "There was a certain creditor who had two debtors. One owed five hundred denarii, and the other fifty. And when they had nothing with which to repay, he **freely forgave them** both. Tell Me, therefore, which of them will love him more?" Simon answered, "I suppose the one whom he forgave more." Jesus said to him, "You have rightly judged."

Then, Jesus turned to the woman and said to Simon, "Do you see this woman? I entered your house; you gave Me no water for My feet, but she has washed My feet with her tears and wiped them with the hair of her head. You gave Me no kiss, but this woman has not ceased to kiss

My feet since the time I came in. You did not anoint My head with oil, but this woman has anointed My feet with fragrant oil. Therefore I say to you, her sins, which are many, are forgiven, for she loved much. But to whom little is forgiven, the same loves little."

The woman loved Jesus **much** because she **knew** that she was **forgiven much**. In actuality, no one has been forgiven little. We have all been forgiven much. As for this woman, she knew it. So the most "dangerous" thing about this doctrine of complete forgiveness of sins is that you will fall in love with Jesus and end up effortlessly fulfilling the greatest commandment: "You shall love the Lord your God with all your heart, with all your soul, and with all your mind" (Matthew 22:36–38). Hallelujah!

If you **think** that you have been forgiven little, then you will love little. But when you **know** the truth of how much you have been forgiven, you will love Jesus much! Knowing how much you have been forgiven is the secret to loving Jesus! In other words, you will only love Jesus much when you experience His lavish grace and unmerited favor in forgiving you of all your sins—past, present and future. But His grace is cheapened when you think that He has only forgiven you of your sins up to the time you got saved, and after that point, you have to depend on your confession of sins to be forgiven.

God's forgiveness is not given in installments. Don't go around thinking that when you confess a sin, He forgives you only for that sin. Then, the next time you sin, you need to confess your sin again for Him to forgive you again. Such is the kind of belief that cheapens His grace. And the result of this is that because you think that He has forgiven you little, you will end up loving Him little, and deprive yourself of running to Him and seeing Him help, deliver and prosper you.

Beloved, with one sacrifice on the cross, Jesus blotted out all the sins of your entire life! Don't cheapen His unmerited favor with your own imperfect efforts to confess all your sins. Accord this gift that Jesus has given you the value that it deserves by fully receiving and experiencing His unmerited favor today!

❖

Father, I thank You that I am forgiven much. In fact, all my sins of my entire life have been forgiven, wiped out once and for all by the eternal blood of Jesus. Therefore, today, I look forward to receiving Your unmerited favor and every good thing You have sent my way!

Today's Thought

Knowing how much I have been forgiven is the secret to loving Jesus much.

Today's Reflection On Favor

_____

_____

_____

_____

_____

_____

_____

_____

_____

_____

_____

_____

_____

_____

_____

_____

DAY 45

Why A Revelation Of Your Forgiveness Is So Important

Today's Scripture

I write to you, little children, because your sins are forgiven you for His name's sake. —1 John 2:12

PEOPLE HAVE ASKED me from time to time, *"Pastor Prince, why is an understanding of the complete forgiveness of my sins so important for me to walk in God's unmerited favor?"*

This is a good question. Let me share with you some of the implications involved. First, if you have no confidence that all your sins have been forgiven, then your eternal security and salvation will always hang in the balance.

When you don't have a clear sense of your complete forgiveness, you will constantly be on an emotional seesaw.

Second, if you think that your sins were not fully dealt with at the cross, then you can never have the confidence to enjoy the Lord's presence because you can never be sure if He is on your side, or if He is waiting to punish you for your failures. You will constantly feel unworthy because of your assessment of your conduct, and you can never really have the boldness to ask God for big things, or believe that He will give you success in your life.

Third, if you do not believe that Jesus has already forgiven all your sins, it means that when you fail, you will believe that you are not "right" with God and that fellowship with Him has been cut off. And instead of depending on His unmerited favor to overcome your failure, you will feel that you need to confess your sin, be remorseful and make amends with God before you can restore fellowship with God and depend on Him again.

It comes down to this: When you don't have a clear sense of your complete forgiveness, you will constantly be on an emotional seesaw. Sometimes, you feel that things between you and God are all right, but at other times, you don't think that it is so. Sometimes, you feel confident that the Lord is with you to make you a success, but at other times, you feel like you blew it and the Lord will not help you until you confess your sin and make amends.

You will be in a constant cycle of feeling insecure, where you are always hopping in and out of God's favor. All these feelings depend on how well you think you have performed, and ignore the cross of Jesus altogether. My friend, God does not evaluate you based on your behavior. He sees only Jesus' perfect work. But because you do not believe that Jesus has indeed forgiven you of all your sins, you end up feeling like a total and complete hypocrite and failure.

I hope that you are beginning to see that understanding the complete forgiveness of your sins is not just for theologians. Thinking that your sins are not completely forgiven will fundamentally affect your relationship with Jesus. While He is all ready to bless you, give you favor and make you a success, unbelief in His finished work robs you of the ability to receive His goodness, His blessings, His unmerited favor and His success in your life.

The cross of Jesus qualified you, but unbelief in the main clause of the new covenant disqualifies you. Meditate on what God says about your sins in the new covenant and free yourself to receive from Him today. The new covenant is based entirely on His unmerited favor. There is nothing for you to do, nothing for you to perform, nothing for you to accomplish. Your part in the new covenant is just to have faith in Jesus and to believe that you are totally forgiven and free to enjoy the new covenant blessings through His finished work!

❖

Today's Prayer

Father, thank You for showing me why it's so important for me to believe that all my sins are forgiven. I don't want my relationship with You to be affected by doubts about my complete forgiveness. I choose to meditate on what You have declared about my sins in the new covenant and see myself receiving all that I need from You today, only because of what Christ has done for me at the cross.

Today's Thought

I am totally forgiven and free to enjoy the new covenant blessings through Jesus' finished work today!

Today's Reflection On Favor

You Can't Lose Fellowship With God

❖

Today's Scripture

*Seventy weeks are determined for your people and for your holy city,
to finish the transgression, to make an end of sins, to make reconciliation
for iniquity, to bring in everlasting righteousness… —Daniel 9:24*

T HERE ARE SOME Christians who believe that you can lose fellowship with God when you sin, and you need to confess your sin to God and obtain forgiveness to become righteous again. They claim that your **relationship** with God is not broken when you sin, but **fellowship** with Him is, so you need to confess your sin to restore fellowship with Him.

**As a new covenant believer, you are righteous not only
until your next sin. You have everlasting righteousness!**

It sounds very good. But believing that your fellowship with God is broken when you sin will affect your ability to come boldly to His throne of grace to receive from Him. In reality, both the words "relationship" and "fellowship" share the same Greek root word *koinonia.*[1] This means that even if you fail, relationship and fellowship with God are not broken. Why? Because your sins and failures have all been paid for at the cross. How can you ever lose your righteousness in Christ when it is based entirely on His perfect work and not your imperfection?

To see how we have everlasting righteousness in Christ, look at the prophecy in the Book of Daniel about Jesus' work at Calvary. Daniel 9:24 describes His mission in no uncertain terms: "…to finish the transgression, to make an end of sins, to make reconciliation for iniquity, to bring in **everlasting righteousness.**" Beloved, we can rejoice today because Jesus has fulfilled every iota of this prophecy! The blood of bulls and goats in the old covenant only provided limited and temporal righteousness for the children of Israel, and that is why with every new failing, the sacrifices had to be repeated.

But in the new covenant, the blood of Jesus put an **end** to sin and gave us everlasting righteousness! Listen carefully to this: Jesus does not have to be crucified repeatedly whenever you fail because every sin has already been paid for on the cross. We need to trust in just how complete and perfect His finished work is. Today, as a new covenant believer, you are righteous not only until your next sin. You have **everlasting righteousness**!

❖

Today's Prayer

Father, I thank You that the blood of Your Son Jesus has put an end to sin and given me everlasting righteousness! And because I have this gift of everlasting righteousness that is not dependent on my works, my fellowship with You cannot be broken even when I mess up. I can still come to you boldly to receive grace and help. How can I not be victorious in life with Your grace and help!

Today's Thought

Because I am in Christ, I have everlasting righteousness!

Today's Reflection On Favor

_____

_____

_____

_____

_____

_____

_____

Our Part In The New Covenant Of Grace

❖

Today's Scripture

Therefore let it be known to you, brethren, that through this Man is preached to you the forgiveness of sins; and by Him everyone who believes is justified from all things from which you could not be justified by the law of Moses.
—*Acts 13:38–39*

WHAT IS OUR part in the new covenant of grace? Our part in the new covenant of grace is to simply **believe**! What should we believe? We are to believe in Jesus! But follow me closely now, this answer may not be as straightforward as it seems. If you were to ask people on the streets if they believed in Jesus, you would probably get all kinds of answers. There would be those who believe that Jesus existed as a historical figure, moral philosopher, charismatic leader or prophet. Sadly, the truth is that believing all these things about Jesus will not save them.

Your part in the new covenant of God's unmerited favor is to believe that you are completely forgiven of all your sins, and that Jesus' blood cleanses you from all your unrighteousness and lawlessness.

So let's establish what it means to believe in Jesus. To believe in Jesus is to first and foremost, believe and receive Him as your personal Lord and Savior who died on the cross for all your sins. To believe in Jesus is to believe that Jesus is the only way to salvation and that once you receive Him, you receive the gift of eternal life. Furthermore, to believe in Jesus is to believe beyond the shadow of a doubt that all your sins—past, present and future—were all punished on the cross and that today (this is where the last clause of the new covenant applies), all your sins and lawless deeds He remembers NO MORE!

Based on the new covenant of grace, what does God want you to believe? He wants you to believe with all your heart that He meant every word when He said, "...I will be merciful to their unrighteousness, and their sins and their lawless deeds I will remember no more" (Hebrews 8:12). You see, in the new covenant, there is nothing for us to do but to believe! Your part in the new covenant of God's unmerited favor is to believe that you are completely forgiven of all your sins, and that Jesus' blood cleanses you from all your unrighteousness and lawlessness.

In God's eyes today, you are made perfectly righteous by Jesus' finished work. The new covenant's emphasis is to believe that you are forgiven of every sin and that God has erased them from His memory. If you don't believe this, it will be impossible for you to depend on and expect God to protect, provide for and prosper you. If you don't believe this, it will rob you of the ability to receive His goodness, blessings, unmerited favor and success in your life. So believe. Only believe!

Today's Prayer

Father, I thank You that all my sins—past, present and future—have been wiped out by the blood of Jesus. You will by no means remember them. Today, I expect to see Your provision and protection. I receive Your goodness, Your blessings, Your unmerited favor and Your good success for every area of my life.

Today's Thought
Only believe!

Today's Reflection On Favor

Test Everything You Hear With God's Word

❖

Today's Scripture

Do not despise prophecies. Test all things; hold fast what is good.
—*1 Thessalonians 5:20–21*

I ENCOURAGE YOU to test everything you hear with God's Word. I always tell my church to read the Bible for themselves instead of simply swallowing all that any preacher, including myself, says. Be wise and don't just swallow everything—hook, line, sinker, fisherman and even his boots! Be discerning when you hear something that does not sit well in your spirit, such as when a preacher tells you that "God gives you sicknesses to teach you a lesson." Ask yourself, "Is this in line with the new covenant of God's unmerited favor? Are there new covenant scriptures to back up this teaching?"

To understand the Bible, we need to read everything in its context.

The answer is obvious once you align it with Jesus and what He has done on the cross for you! Why would God give you sicknesses when Jesus has taken every sickness and disease upon His own body at the cross? With full assurance in your heart that sickness is not from God, you can have faith to be healed! But what assurance can you have if you believe the lie that the condition is from God? Now, instead of thinking that God is against you, you realize that He is on your side! Your confidence is restored, faith is renewed and His healing can flow unabated through every cell, tissue and organ in your body!

Let me just share with you the words of Miles Coverdale, who said, "It shall greatly help thee to understand scripture, if thou mark not only what is spoken or written, but of whom, and unto whom, with what words, at what time, where, to what intent, with what circumstance, considering what goeth before, and what followeth after."[1]

Essentially, he was saying that to understand the Bible, we need to read everything in its context. What powerful advice from the man who translated and produced the first English Bible in the 16th century.

My friend, rightly divide the covenants whenever you read the Bible and you will never be ashamed. Now that you have received Jesus into your life, you are under the new covenant and it is your new covenant right to enjoy Jesus' unmerited favor to succeed in life!

Today's Prayer

Father, give me a discerning heart so that when I read my Bible or listen to a sermon, I will know what is of the old covenant and what is of the new covenant. I don't want to be gullible or naive, Father, but I want to be able to recognize what is on Your heart for me today, and what is merely man's opinion or tradition, so that I may enjoy with confidence Your unmerited favor that is based on the truth of Your Word.

Today's Thought

It is my new covenant right to enjoy Jesus' unmerited favor to succeed in life.

Today's Reflection On Favor

_____

_____

_____

_____

_____

_____

Put The Spotlight On Jesus' Finished Work

Today's Scripture

I was alive once without the law, but when the commandment came, sin revived and I died. And the commandment, which was to bring life, I found to bring death. —Romans 7:9–10

Iɴ 1942, C S Lewis wrote a brilliant book entitled *The Screwtape Letters*. It tells the story of a senior demon teaching a junior demon how to exploit man's weaknesses and frailties. Along the same lines, I would imagine that Romans 7:9 is probably the most studied and memorized verse in hell. All junior demons would be taught this verse and the lecture would be titled, "How to bring about a revival of sin"! According to Paul, when you introduce the law, there will be a REVIVAL OF SIN! And that's not all. Apart from reviving sin, the law also kills and brings death! Isn't it amazing, then, that there are well-meaning ministers who preach strongly on the Ten Commandments, thinking that imposing the law would cause sin to be removed?

The only way out of the vicious circle of defeat is to put the spotlight on the finished work of Jesus.

According to Romans 3:20, **"by the law is the knowledge of sin."** In other words, without the law, there would be no knowledge of sin. For instance, you can drive at any speed that you like on a road that doesn't have a speed limit and nobody can accuse you of speeding. But once the authorities put a speed limit on the same road, you now have the knowledge that if you drive beyond say, 70 miles an hour on this road, you would be breaking the law.

In the same way, Paul said, "For I would not have known covetousness unless the law had said, 'You shall not covet'" (Romans 7:7). That is why the enemy always pours accusations on you using the voice of a legalist. He uses the law and the commandments to show up your failures, to put a spotlight on how your behavior has disqualified you from fellowship with God, and to constantly point out how you are undeserving of His acceptance, love and blessings! The enemy uses the law to heap condemnation upon you and give you a sense of guilt and distance from God. He knows that the more condemnation and guilt you experience, the more likely you are to feel alienated from God and to continue in that sin. The only way out of this vicious circle of defeat is to put the spotlight on the finished work of Jesus, who by His death at the cross took your condemnation and qualified you to receive God's acceptance, love and blessings forevermore.

Today's Prayer

Father, I thank You that there is no condemnation for me because I am in Christ. I thank You that my sins are forgiven and You see me righteous in Christ. Help me to always remember these eternal truths, especially when the enemy tries to use the law to condemn me. I thank You that today and every day, I have Your constant presence, love and acceptance.

Today's Thought

The enemy's favorite weapon to keep me defeated is the law. So I'll put the spotlight on Jesus' finished work and not my self-effort.

Today's Reflection On Favor

_____

_____

_____

_____

_____

God's Robust Peace

❖

Today's Scripture

...the peace of God, which surpasses all understanding, will guard your hearts and minds through Christ Jesus. —Philippians 4:7

I WANT TO talk to you today about experiencing God's kind of peace in the midst of fearful circumstances. My friend, peace is not the absence of trouble in your life. It is not the absence of turmoil, challenges or things that are not harmonious in your physical environment. It is possible to be in the midst of the biggest crisis in your life and still experience peace. That's the true kind of peace that you can experience with Jesus—peace that surpasses understanding. Naturally speaking, it does not make sense for you to feel completely at rest and at peace when you are in dire straits, but supernaturally, you can be filled with peace!

Jesus gives us peace, security, covering and protection even in the midst of a storm.

The world defines peace, harmony and tranquility based on what is happening in the sensory realm. The world's notion of peace would look something like this: A man lying in a hammock on a white sandy beach in Hawaii with luau music playing softly in the cabana, coconut trees swaying in perfect unison and warm, blue waves rolling languidly along the shoreline. The world calls that peace—until reality kicks in, and the transient peace that was experienced just moments ago dissipates into thin air!

You see, my friend, you cannot use your external surroundings to permanently influence the turmoil that you are feeling inside. Only Jesus can touch what you are feeling inside and turn that turmoil into His peace. With the Lord by your side, and from that abiding peace within, you can influence your external surroundings. It's not the other way round. With Jesus, transformation is always from inside out and not outside in. He puts a peace and rest in your heart that is so secure, you can face any challenge without worry or stress, regardless of your negative circumstances and environment.

Today's Prayer

Father, I acknowledge that the kind of peace the world offers cannot last. Show me today and in the days to come how I can experience and walk more in Your deep, abiding peace that surpasses all understanding, that is mine in Christ.

Today's Thought

God's inward peace can influence my outward circumstances.

Today's Reflection On Favor

_____

_____

_____

_____

_____

_____

_____

_____

_____

_____

_____

_____

Peace In The Midst Of A Storm

❖

Today's Scripture

He who dwells in the secret place of the Most High shall abide under the shadow of the Almighty…He shall cover you with His feathers, and under His wings you shall take refuge… —Psalm 91:1, 4

I REMEMBER READING about an art competition where the theme given was "peace." The artist who most effectively depicted peace in his artwork would win the competition. The artists gathered their paints, canvases and brushes and started creating their masterpieces. When the time came to judge the artworks, the judges were impressed by the various scenes of tranquility illustrated by the artists. There was a majestic piece capturing the brilliance of the sun setting over lush greenery, one that depicted a serene landscape of moonlit hills and another evocative piece that showed a lone man walking leisurely through a rustic paddy field.

Only Jesus can touch what you are feeling inside and turn that turmoil into His peace.

Then, the judges came upon a peculiar piece that looked almost horrifying and perhaps even ugly to some. It was the very antithesis of every other piece that the judges had seen. It was a wild cacophony of violent colors and the aggression with which the artist had lashed his brush against the canvas was obvious. It depicted a raging storm where the ocean waves were swollen to menacing heights and slamming against the craggy edges of a cliff with thunderous force. Lightning zigzagged across the blackened sky and the branches of the single tree that was perched atop the cliff were all swept to the side by the force of the gale. Now, how could this picture be the epitome of peace?

Yet, the judges unanimously awarded the first prize to the artist who painted the turbulent storm. While the results initially appeared to be appalling, the judges' decision immediately became clear once you give the winning canvas a closer look. Hidden in a crevice in the cliff is a family of eagles snug in their nest. The mother eagle faces the blustering winds, but her young chicks are oblivious to the storm and have dozed off under the shelter of her wings.

Now, **that's** the kind of peace that Jesus gives to you and me! He gives us peace, security, covering and protection even in the midst of a storm. The psalmist describes this beautifully: "He who dwells in the secret place of the Most High shall abide under the shadow of the Almighty...He shall cover you with His feathers, and under His wings you shall take refuge."

There is no safer place than under the protective shelter of your Savior's wings. It does not matter what circumstances may be raging around you. You can cry to the Lord for His unmerited favor, as David did in Psalm 57:1—"Be merciful to me, O God, be merciful to me! For my soul trusts in You; and in the shadow of Your wings I will make my refuge, until these calamities have passed by." The New American Standard Bible says, "Be gracious to me, O God, be gracious to me, for my soul takes refuge in You; and in the shadow of Your wings I will take refuge until destruction passes by." What blessed assurance we can have today, knowing that even if destruction rages around us, we can take refuge in the Lord.

❖

Today's Prayer

Father, I thank You that in the midst of any crisis, I can take refuge in the shadow of Your wings and have Your peace. My trust is in You and I thank You that You will protect and deliver me and all my loved ones no matter what is raging around us.

Today's Thought

Come what may, I can take refuge in
the Lord and enjoy His peace.

Today's Reflection On Favor

_____

_____

_____

_____

_____

_____

_____

_____

_____

_____

_____

_____

_____

_____

_____

_____

_____

_____

_____

Guard What Comes Through Your Eye- And Ear-Gates

❖

Today's Scripture

My son, give attention to my words; incline your ear to my sayings.
Do not let them depart from your eyes; keep them in the midst of your
heart; for they are life to those who find them, and health to all their flesh.
—Proverbs 4:20–22

I WAS WATCHING a popular program on television with the host of that program interviewing some experts about the economy in America. One "expert" was very positive and gave his reasons for being so upbeat. Then, another "expert" interjected and gave his reasons for a bleak economic outlook. I watched this program for over an hour and none of these "experts" agreed on anything in the end.

The more we hear and see Jesus, the healthier and stronger we become! Our mortal bodies become infused with His resurrection life and power!

The thing about such discussions, be it on television, the papers or the Internet, is that it's supposed to present two sides—one good and the other bad. No real solution or resolution is actually offered. Sometime after watching that program, I shared with my pastoral team that I realized that I had unknowingly been feeding on the tree of the knowledge of good and evil. That's all I got from watching such programs—more knowledge of what was good and what was evil, but this knowledge did nothing for me.

On the other hand, when we feed on the person of Jesus, who is the tree of life, we find that His wisdom, understanding, peace, joy and unmerited favor will flow in our lives! Again, I am not saying that you should not watch the news. I am just saying that it is important for you to watch your viewing diet. It is far more powerful to be full of Jesus than to be full of worldly knowledge.

I always encourage my church to be mindful of their eye- and ear-gates. Essentially, this means that we need to be conscious of what we watch and hear on a regular basis. The Book of Proverbs, which is chock-full of God's wisdom, tells us, "My son, **give attention to my words**; incline **your ear** to my sayings. Do not let them depart from **your eyes**; keep them in the midst of **your heart**; for they are **life** to those who find them, and **health** to all their flesh."

God tells us to guard what we **hear**, what we **see** and what is **in our hearts**. He wants us to have our ears full of the gracious words of Jesus, our eyes full of the presence of Jesus and our hearts meditating on what we have heard and seen in Jesus. That's what "give attention to my words" means today in the new covenant, for Jesus is God's Word made flesh. John 1:14 says, "And the Word became flesh and dwelt among us, and we beheld His glory, the glory as of the only begotten of the Father, full of grace [unmerited favor] and truth."

It is all about beholding Jesus, and as we behold Him, we are transformed more and more into His likeness, full of unmerited favor and truth! Don't miss this powerful promise, my friend. The result of tuning our ear- and eye-gates to Jesus is that He will be **life** and **health** to us. The Bible shows us that there is a direct correlation between hearing and seeing Jesus, and the health of our physical bodies. The more we hear and see Jesus, the healthier and stronger we become! Our mortal bodies become infused with His resurrection life and power!

If we are constantly feeding on the news media, it is no wonder that we feel weak and tired. There is just no nourishment for us there. Please hear what I am saying. It is all right to keep yourself abreast of current world events and be in the know about what is happening in the Middle

East, trends in the economy and developments in the political arena. Such information may even be necessary for the industry that you are in. I am not asking you to become an ignoramus or to live in a cave. What I am saying is this: Know what is good for the wholeness of your body and mind. Be wise—don't overdose yourself on information and knowledge that does not infuse you with God's life and power.

Today's Prayer

Father, help me to be wise in guarding what I let in through my eye- and ear-gates. I ask You to create in me a hunger for more of Jesus and His Word. I want my eyes to always behold His beauty and my ears to always hear His gracious words. And as I see and hear more of Jesus by Your Holy Spirit, I thank You for a greater measure of peace, wholeness and strength flowing through my body and soul.

Today's Thought

The more I behold Jesus, the more I become saturated in His unmerited favor.

Today's Reflection On Favor

_____

_____

_____

_____

_____

_____

_____

_____

_____

Receive Jesus' Shalom

❖

Today's Scripture

A heart at peace gives life to the body... —*Proverbs 14:30* NIV

THE BEST WAY to know if you are embroiled in the things of the world is to be objective and ask yourself this: "Is my heart troubled?" I believe that the number one killer in the modern world is **stress**. Medical doctors in my church have told me that if a patient has high blood pressure, they can advise the patient to cut down on sodium. They can also advise their patients to cut down on other excesses such as sugar or cholesterol. But as doctors, there is one thing that they cannot control in their patients, and that is their patients' stress levels.

Stress is not from God. Peace is from Him!

I personally believe that the physical root cause of many medical conditions today is stress. Stress can produce all kinds of imbalances in your body. It can cause you to age prematurely, give you rashes, cause gastric pains and even lead to abnormal growths in your body. To put it succinctly, stress kills! Doctors tell us that certain physical symptoms are "psychosomatic" in nature. That's because these symptoms are brought about by psychological problems such as stress. Stress is not from God. **Peace** is from Him!

I trust that you are beginning to understand why Jesus said, "Peace I leave with you, My peace I give to you; not as the world gives do I give to you. Let not your heart be troubled, neither let it be afraid" (John 14:27). Now, Jesus would not have used the word "peace." The Greek New Testament renders "peace" as *eirene*, but since Jesus spoke

Aramaic-Hebrew, He would have used the word "shalom"—"**Shalom** I leave with you, My **shalom** I give to you; not as the world gives do I give to you."

In the Hebrew vernacular, "shalom" is a very rich and loaded word. There is no English word that can accurately encapsulate the fullness, richness and power contained in the word "shalom." Hence, English Bible translators were only able to translate it as "peace." But while the word "shalom" includes peace, it means so much more. Let's look at the Brown Driver & Briggs Hebrew Lexicon to get a better idea of what Jesus meant when He said, "Shalom I leave with you."

The Hebrew Lexicon describes "shalom" as **completeness, safety, soundness (in body), welfare, health, prosperity, peace, quiet, tranquility, contentment, peace used of human relationships, peace with God especially in our covenant relationship and peace from war.**[1] Wow, what a powerful word! This is the shalom that Jesus has bequeathed you: His completeness, His safety, His soundness, His welfare, His health, His prosperity, His peace, His quietness, His tranquility, His contentment, His peace in human relationships, His peace with God through the covenant made at the cross and His peace from war. All these, my friend, are part of your inheritance in Christ today!

Can you picture the full implications of what it means to experience Jesus' shalom in your life? Can you picture your life being free from regrets, anxieties and worries? How healthy, vibrant, energetic and strong you will be! Thank Him for this blessing today and start enjoying Jesus' shalom in every area of your life.

❖

Lord Jesus, thank You for giving me Your shalom in every area of my life. I want to experience and walk in a greater measure of Your shalom. I want to live a life that is free of regrets, anxieties and worries, and experience more of Your health, energy and strength. Today, because I have Your shalom, I will walk in Your peace, prosperity and protection as I deal with the demands of this day.

Today's Thought

Less stress plus more of Jesus' shalom equals more health.

Today's Reflection On Favor

DAY 54

Jesus' Peace Sets You Up For Success

❖

Today's Scripture

There is no fear in love; but perfect love casts out fear, because fear involves torment. But he who fears has not been made perfect in love.
—*1 John 4:18*

JESUS GIVES YOU His shalom to set you up for success in life. You cannot be a success in your marriage, family and career when you are crippled and paralyzed with fear. Today, as you are reading this, I believe with all my heart that Jesus has already begun a work in your heart to liberate you from all your fears, whatever they may be. They may be the fear of failure, the fear of success, the fear of people's opinions of you or even the fear that God is not with you.

Jesus' shalom is on your side to make you a success in life.

All the fears that you are experiencing in your life today began with an untruth, a lie that you have somehow believed. Perhaps you have believed that God is angry and displeased with you, and that His presence is far from you. That's why the Bible says, "There is no fear in love; but perfect love casts out fear, because fear involves torment. But he who fears has not been made perfect in love."

This scripture tells us that when you begin to have a revelation that God loves you perfectly (not because of what you have accomplished, but because of what Jesus has accomplished for you), that revelation of the unmerited favor of Jesus will cast out every fear, every lie, every anxiety, every doubt and every worry that God is against you. The more you have a revelation of Jesus and how He has made you perfect, the more you will free yourself to receive His complete shalom and succeed in life!

My friend, know that as a believer in Jesus Christ, you have absolute peace with God. The new covenant of grace is also known as the covenant of peace. Today, you stand upon the righteousness of Jesus and not your own. Today, because of Jesus, God says this to you: "I would not be angry with you, nor rebuke [condemn] you. For the mountains shall depart and the hills be removed, but My kindness shall not depart from you, nor shall My **covenant of peace** be removed" (Isaiah 54:9–10).

God is on your side. Jesus' shalom is on your side to make you a success in life. All of heaven's resources are on your side. Even if you are caught in the midst of a storm right now, just think of the picture of the eagle chicks sleeping soundly in spite of the storm, nestled under the wings of their mother, their protector and provider. And may the shalom of God, which surpasses all understanding, guard your heart and mind through Christ Jesus (Philippians 4:7). Go in this peace, my friend, and rest upon His shalom!

❖

Today's Prayer

Father, give me a greater revelation of how perfectly You love me, for Your perfect love will cast out every fear in my life. You don't want me fearful of failure, of people's opinions of me or of what the future may hold. Because of Jesus, I am in a covenant of grace and peace where I will always experience Your kindness, and where the shalom of Jesus is always on my side to make me a success in life!

Today's Thought

God is not angry with me. He does not condemn me, but loves me perfectly because of Jesus' perfect sacrifice for me.

Today's Reflection On Favor

_____

_____

_____

_____

DAY 55

Grace And Truth Are One

❖

Today's Scripture

For the law was given through Moses, but grace [unmerited favor]
and truth came through Jesus Christ. —John 1:17

Dɪᴅ ʏᴏᴜ ᴋɴᴏᴡ that God sees grace (unmerited favor) and truth as one and the same thing? Notice in John 1:17 that truth is on the same side as God's unmerited favor and both grace (unmerited favor) and truth came through Jesus Christ. When I did a study of this verse in its original Greek, I found out that "grace and truth" are actually referred to as a singular unit, since they are followed by the singular verb translated as "came." In other words, in God's eyes, grace and truth are synonymous—unmerited favor is truth and truth is unmerited favor.

You cannot separate truth from grace and grace from truth
as they are both embodied in the person of Jesus Christ.

Sometimes, people tell me things like, "Well, it's good that you preach grace, but we also have to tell people about truth." This makes it seem as though grace and truth are two different things when, in fact, they are one and the same. You cannot separate truth from grace and grace from truth as they are both embodied in the person of Jesus Christ. In fact, just a few verses before this, John 1:14, referring to the person of Jesus, says, "And the Word became flesh and dwelt among us, and we beheld His glory, the glory as of the only begotten of the Father, **full of grace [unmerited favor] and truth**." Grace and truth **came** together through the person and ministry of Jesus. Grace is not a doctrine or teaching. Grace is a Person.

This is contrasted with the old covenant of law that was **given** through Moses on Mount Sinai. We can see that God is very precise in dealing with the two covenants and does not mix them together. Grace is grace and law is law. Grace came by Jesus whereas the law was given through Moses. Jesus didn't come to give us more laws. He came to give us His unmerited favor, which is His truth! It would be of immense profit to you to keep in mind that every time you read the word "grace" in the Bible, you translate it mentally as "unmerited favor," because that is what it is.

My friend, "grace came." It is one thing to give, but it is another thing to come. You see, I could send a DVD of my sermon to you instead of coming to you. But if I come to you, it's personal. The law was given by Moses, but grace came by Jesus Christ. Every system of morality is about man trying to reach God with his discipline and good works, but in Christianity, God came down to where we were to lift us up to where He is!

Today's Prayer

Father, I thank You that Jesus came personally to die for me and set me free from sin, bondages and eternal death. I thank You that He didn't come to give me more laws, but to give me Your unmerited favor, which is Your truth. Today, I have been lifted up and am seated with Christ at Your right hand, all because grace came!

Today's Thought

Jesus didn't come to give me more laws. He came to give me His unmerited favor, which is His truth.

Today's Reflection On Favor

_____

_____

_____

_____

DAY 56

Blessed Because Of God's Goodness

❖

Today's Scripture

And the Lord spoke to Moses, saying, "I have heard the complaints of the children of Israel. Speak to them, saying, 'At twilight you shall eat meat, and in the morning you shall be filled with bread. And you shall know that I am the Lord your God.'" —Exodus 16:11–12

MANY YEARS AGO, when I was studying God's Word, the Lord spoke to me, saying, "Before the law was given, none of the children of Israel died when they came out of Egypt. Even though they murmured and complained against God's appointed leadership, not a single one of them died. This is a picture of pure grace." I had never heard anyone teach this before or read it in any book, so I quickly went through that portion in my Bible and indeed, I could not find anyone who died before the law was given!

Living under grace means that all the blessings and provisions that we receive are dependent on God's goodness and not our obedience.

God had delivered the children of Israel from a lifetime of slavery by performing great signs and wonders. But when they found themselves caught between the Red Sea and the advancing Egyptian army, they complained to Moses, saying, "Because there were no graves in Egypt, have you taken us away to die in the wilderness? Why have you so dealt with us, to bring us up out of Egypt?" (Exodus 14:11). What audacity! And yet, did God punish those who murmured? No, in fact, He saved the Israelites spectacularly, opening up the Red Sea for them to escape from their pursuers who were closing in on them.

After they had crossed over to the other side of the Red Sea, they continued to murmur over and over again, in spite of God's miraculous provisions and gracious protection. At a place called Marah, they complained that the waters were bitter and God made the waters sweet and refreshing for them (Exodus 15:23–25). Then, when they had no food, they grumbled to Moses again, saying, "Oh, that we had died by the hand of the Lord in the land of Egypt, when we sat by the pots of meat and when we ate bread to the full! For you have brought us out into this wilderness to kill this whole assembly with hunger" (Exodus 16:3). Their ungrateful diatribes were directed not only at Moses, but also at God. So did God rain fire and brimstone on them? No! He rained bread from heaven to feed them! It was as if every fresh murmuring brought forth fresh demonstrations of God's goodness!

Do you know why?

It is because all these events occurred before the Ten Commandments were given. You see, before the law was given, the children of Israel lived under grace (unmerited favor). Living under grace meant that all the blessings and provisions that they received were dependent on God's goodness and not their obedience. The Lord delivered them out of Egypt not because of their goodness or good behavior. He brought them out by the blood of the lamb (a picture of the blood of the Lamb of God) that was applied on their doorposts on the night of the first Passover.

The children of Israel were dependent upon God's faithfulness to the Abrahamic covenant, which was a covenant based on His grace (unmerited favor). Abraham lived more than 400 years before the law was given, long before there were the Ten Commandments. God had related to Abraham based on Abraham's faith in His grace and not based on Abraham's obedience to the law. God's Word makes it clear that Abraham was not justified by the law: "For if Abraham was justified by works, he has something to boast about, but not before God. For what does the Scripture say? 'Abraham **believed** God, and it was **accounted to him for righteousness**'" (Romans 4:2–3). How was Abraham made righteous? He believed God and it was accounted to him for righteousness!

When the Israelites journeyed from Egypt to Mount Sinai, they were under the Abrahamic covenant of grace. Therefore, in spite of their sins, God delivered them out of Egypt and provided for them supernaturally, **not based on their goodness and faithfulness, but based on His goodness and faithfulness.** The good news for you and me is this: Today, we are under the new covenant of grace (unmerited favor), and God's unmerited favor is upon us. His blessings and His provisions for us are based entirely on HIS GOODNESS and HIS FAITHFULNESS. Hallelujah! How cool is that?

Today's Prayer

Father, I thank You for all the times You have blessed me despite my complaints and lack of faith. I am so glad that You bless me not because of my goodness or faithfulness, but because of Your goodness and faithfulness. I call this day blessed, fruitful and full of Your free favors because I am under Your pure grace!

Today's Thought

God blesses me not because of my goodness and faithfulness, but because of HIS goodness and faithfulness!

Today's Reflection On Favor

_____

_____

_____

_____

_____

_____

The Power To Sin No More

❖

Today's Scripture

Therefore there is now no condemnation for those who are in Christ Jesus.
—*Romans 8:1* NASB

TODAY, I WANT to talk about how you can have a victorious thought life. My friend, the solution to temptations, sinful desires and thoughts is found in the very first verse of Romans 8: "Therefore there is now no condemnation for those who are in Christ Jesus." (By the way, some Bible translations, like the New King James Version, go on to say "who do not walk according to the flesh, but according to the Spirit." This was added by the later Bible translators. In the oldest manuscripts of the New Testament available today, the Greek simply states, "There is therefore now no condemnation for those who are in Christ Jesus.")

You now have the power of Christ to rise above your temptation and to rest in your righteous identity in Christ apart from your works.

You may experience temptations and sinful thoughts from time to time, but right in the midst of that temptation, you need to know this: There **is** therefore **now** no condemnation for those who are in Christ Jesus. Notice that this verse is in the present tense. Right now, even if at this very moment, sinful thoughts are going through your mind, there is no condemnation because you are IN CHRIST JESUS! Are we then to sit still and entertain those sinful thoughts? Of course not.

Sin cannot take root in a person who is full of the consciousness that he is righteous in Christ. You cannot stop birds from flying over your

155

head, but you can certainly stop a bird from building a nest on your head. In the same way, you cannot stop temptations, sinful thoughts and desires from passing through your mind, but you can certainly stop yourself from **acting** on these temptations, sinful thoughts and desires. How? By confessing at the very moment of temptation that you are the righteousness of God in Christ Jesus!

The power of Jesus to overcome every temptation kicks in when you remain conscious that even at the point of temptation, Jesus is **still** with you and that you are righteous in Him apart from your works (Romans 4:6)! When you do that, you reject the condemnation for the temptation that you faced. You now have the power of Christ to rise above your temptation and to rest in your righteous identity in Christ apart from your works. That, beloved, is the overcoming life in Christ!

Today's Prayer

Father, I thank You that because I am in Christ Jesus, I have the overcoming life. I also have Your unmerited favor because I am righteous in Christ, who is always with me. It is Your goodness and grace that will help me triumph over every challenge today.

Today's Thought

I choose not to be sin-conscious, but conscious of the fact that I am righteous in Christ.

Today's Reflection On Favor

_____

_____

_____

_____

_____

_____

Freedom From Destructive Habits

❖

Today's Scripture
...And Jesus said to her, "Neither do I condemn you; go and sin no more."
—John 8:11

I HAVE RECEIVED so many testimonies from people who have been set free from destructive habits. These are sincere and precious people who desired to experience breakthroughs but did not know how to. However, once they learned about righteousness that comes from Christ apart from their works, they began to confess that they were still the righteousness of God every time they felt tempted. And bit by bit, the more they started to believe that they were righteous in Christ, and the more they refused to accept the condemnation for their past mistakes and for their present temptation, the more they became set free from the very addictions that bound them!

As Jesus is spotless and without blame, so are you in Christ!

A brother from the US, who has been listening to my messages for some time, wrote to share that he had been addicted to pornography and had lived a lifestyle of sexual immorality since he was 14 years old. Although he had accepted Jesus when he was 18 years old, he continued to struggle with this aspect of his life. This is what he wrote:

As a result of some bad influences and some of my own bad choices, I became a pornography addict and began to lead a sexually immoral life at the age of 14. I got saved when I was 18 years old, but I still struggled with those kinds of thoughts and some old, bad habits. I tried everything to break free from immorality and lustful thoughts.

Then, I heard Pastor Prince's message titled, "Good Things Happen To People Who Believe God Loves Them." I listened to it over and over again, and for the first time, God's love became consistently real to me. I was able to receive God's unconditional love over and over again, and it healed my heart.

God's love has set me free*! Thank you so much for the message that your church sends out to the world. It is truly changing lives!*

The revelation that God loves him **unconditionally** despite his failures and imperfections was what helped this brother break free from habits that had gripped him for many years. Beloved, God does **not** want you to sin because sin will destroy you. But even if you have failed, you must know this: There is no condemnation because you are IN CHRIST JESUS and your sins are washed away by His blood! When God looks at you, He does not see you in your failures. From the moment you accepted Jesus as your personal Lord and Savior, God sees you **in** the risen Christ, seated at His right hand! As Jesus is spotless and without blame, so are you! God sent His Son to die on the cross for you **while** you were still a sinner. Obviously, He does not love you only when you are perfect in your behavior and thoughts. His love for you is unconditional. Receive it afresh today and break free from every sin and addiction in your life!

❖

Today's Prayer

Father, I thank You that the power to overcome every challenge today is mine because I am righteous in Christ. Thank You for the gifts of righteousness and no condemnation. I know that my sins cannot stop Your grace, but Your unmerited favor working in my life will enable me to walk in victory in every situation.

Today's Thought

Knowing and believing that God does not condemn me even when I have sinned empowers me to overcome that sin.

Today's Reflection On Favor

_____

_____

_____

_____

_____

_____

_____

_____

_____

_____

_____

_____

_____

_____

_____

_____

_____

_____

_____

_____

_____

DAY 59

The Power Of Jesus' Blood

❖

Today's Scripture

In Him we have redemption through His blood, the forgiveness of sins, according to the riches of His grace. —Ephesians 1:7

Y OU MAY ASK, if God is all-knowing, how can He possibly forget all our sins? Under the new covenant, God can declare that He will no longer remember your sins because your sins were already remembered in the body of Jesus at the cross. My friend, there is one thing that God cannot do—He cannot lie. So He **means** it when He says that He will remember your sins no more. Our part in the new covenant of God's unmerited favor is to **believe** that God indeed remembers our sins no more!

If the enemy can get you to believe the lie that you are not completely forgiven, and keep you sin-conscious, he will be able to keep you defeated, condemned, fearful of God and caught in a vicious circle of failure.

There is power in the blood of Jesus to forgive you from all your sins! The enemy fears this truth the most and that is why he attacks this teaching on the forgiveness of sins so vehemently. If the enemy can get you to believe the lie that you are not completely forgiven and keep you sin-conscious, he will be able to keep you defeated, condemned, fearful of God and caught in a vicious circle of failure.

The writings of the Gnostics are malevolent because they propagate the lie that Jesus was a mere mortal, which means that His blood has no power to cleanse us from all our sins. This is a lie from the pit of hell! Jesus is the Son of God and His blood is untainted by any sin. That is why the shedding of His pure and innocent blood is able to cleanse us from all unrighteousness. His blood does not cover sins temporarily like the blood of bulls and goats in the old covenant. His blood blots out and **completely erases** all our sins. This is the blood of God Himself, shed for the forgiveness of all our sins! We need to start to realize that this is not a "basic teaching." This **is** the gospel of Jesus Christ.

In the end times, people will not be anti-God, but they will be anti-Christ. The anti-Christ movement in the end times will attempt to devalue Jesus' deity, the cross and His power to forgive all our sins. That is why, in these last days, we need more preaching about Jesus, His finished work and the new covenant of His unmerited favor. We need more new covenant, Christ-centered preachers who will put the cross of Jesus as the focus of all their preaching. The only way to stem this deception from creeping into the church is to focus on exalting the person of Jesus and the central tenet of the new covenant, which is the complete forgiveness of sins! This is the gospel and when the gospel truth is preached, people will be set free.

There should be no compromise when it comes to the gospel of Jesus. Forgiveness of sins is based on His grace (unmerited favor) alone and we have access into this grace by **faith**. Our part is to only believe! This is what makes the gospel the good news. Take away the complete forgiveness of sins and it is no longer the "gospel," which means "good news." Beloved, believe that all your sins are forgiven. That is your part in the new covenant. That is how you become established in the new covenant of grace and experience the fullness of His unmerited favor!

❖

Today's Prayer

Father, I thank You that Jesus' blood is not like the blood of bulls and goats, which can never take away sins permanently. I thank You that His blood is eternal and has the power to remove all my sins—past, present and future—once and for all! Today, I stand before You totally forgiven forevermore. As Jesus is without any blemish of sin, so am I in Your sight!

Today's Thought

Because Jesus' blood has cleansed me completely, I expect to experience the fullness of His unmerited favor today.

Today's Reflection On Favor

_____

_____

_____

_____

_____

_____

_____

_____

_____

_____

_____

_____

_____

_____

_____

_____

_____

_____

DAY 60

Come As You Are To Jesus

❖

Today's Scripture

You have turned for me my mourning into dancing; You have put off my sackcloth and clothed me with gladness. —Psalm 30:11

MY FRIEND, YOU are favored and accepted by God today because of **His** unmerited favor. Even if your life is a mess, He can take your mess and make it into something beautiful. Come to Him just as you are.

Years ago, one of my church members suddenly stopped coming to church for a long time. I met up with him to find out how he was doing and to see if everything was alright. He was very honest with me and told me that he was going through a lot of problems in his marriage, and that he was now addicted to alcohol. Then, he said this: "Let me get my life right, then I will come back to church."

You are made holy, righteous and clean by the blood of Jesus Christ, and it is His righteous standing that qualifies you—nothing more and nothing less.

I smiled and asked him, "Do you clean yourself before you take a bath?" I could tell from his expression that he was taken aback by my question, so I told him, "Come **as you are** to the Lord. He is the bath. He will cleanse you. He will get your life in order for you, and He will cause every addiction to lose its hold on you. You don't have to use your own efforts to clean yourself before you take a bath!"

I am glad to share that this precious brother soon returned to church and Jesus turned his life around. Today, he is happily married, blessed with a beautiful family and is one of my trusted, key leaders. That is what the Lord does when you come to Him as you are, and allow Him to love you into wholeness. He will make all things beautiful in your life.

There are many people today who are like this brother. They want to get their lives together by themselves before they come to Jesus. They are under the impression that they need to make themselves holy before they can step into God's holy presence. They feel like they are being hypocrites if they don't sort out their lives first before coming to church.

Nothing could be further from the truth. You will **never** be able to make yourself holy enough to qualify for God's blessings. You are made holy, righteous and clean by the blood of Jesus Christ, and it is **His** righteous standing that qualifies you—nothing more and nothing less. So stop trying to clean yourself before you go to the Lord. Come to Jesus with all your mess, all your addictions, all your weaknesses and all your failures. God loves you just as you are. However, He also loves you too much to let you stay the same. My friend, when you come to Jesus, He becomes your "bath." He will wash you clean, whiter than snow! Jump into the bath today and allow Jesus to make you perfect, righteous and holy in God's eyes!

❖

Today's Prayer

Lord Jesus, Your grace saves the worst of us. No matter how messed up my life is, You can turn it around and make it beautiful. I come to You just as I am today, with all my faults and failings. I thank You that You have made me righteous with Your blood and that You are washing me with the water of Your Word and loving me into wholeness once more. Your unmerited favor in my life will remove every addiction and sickness, turn my mourning into rejoicing and fill my heart with Your robust peace!

Today's Thought

No one cleans himself before taking a bath. So I'll come to Jesus—the bath—just as I am.

Today's Reflection On Favor

_____

_____

_____

_____

_____

_____

_____

_____

_____

_____

_____

_____

_____

_____

_____

_____

_____

_____

_____

_____

_____

DAY 61

Won Over By God's Grace

❖

Today's Scripture

For sin shall not have dominion over you, for you are not under law but under grace. —Romans 6:14

A DEAR SISTER from my church wrote to share about how the Lord had thoroughly transformed her life. She used to frequent nightclubs and pubs regularly, spout vulgarities, take drugs, stay away from home, and get involved in illegal activities such as theft and peddling pirated software.

It is vital for you to receive the gift of no condemnation because that is what will give you the power to overcome your weaknesses, destructive habits and addictions.

During this time, she was often depressed and even entertained thoughts of suicide. Finally, she hit rock bottom and felt that everything in her life had gone wrong. She could hardly convince herself to live on. It was during this period that her sister brought her to New Creation Church and she was impacted by the gospel of grace. This is her testimony:

*I was introduced to grace for the first time and **I learned that God does not despise or condemn delinquents like myself**...I was amazed as I began to see Christianity from a new light for the first time.*

To cut a long story short, I challenged the Lord one day to prove His existence and love for me and He did just that. Within a span of two weeks, I was completely won over by Jesus and gladly accepted Him into my life. As what people always say, the rest is history.

*I would like to testify that it was GRACE and not the LAW that drew a great sinner like me to God. Over time, the Lord transformed me from a delinquent into a lady who is so in love with Jesus! He did not modify my outward behavior immediately when I was still a baby Christian. Instead, **He poured His love and grace abundantly into my life, which eventually transformed me from the inside out**. Grace may not produce immediate results, but the fruits are sure and permanent!*

Just when my family members had given up their hopes on me, my Daddy God did a miracle by changing me effortlessly from within into a new person! Everyone around me marveled at the change when they saw the works of God in my life. I am a walking testimony of God's existence and grace! Hallelujah!

Praise the Lord, isn't this an awesome testimony? This sister was rescued at the lowest point in her life because she realized one powerful truth—God does not despise or condemn her. He LOVES her and it was this revelation of His love and grace (unmerited favor) that turned her life around completely!

Beloved, it is vital for you to receive the gift of no condemnation because that is what will give you the power to overcome your weaknesses, destructive habits and addictions. If you believe that God condemns you for your failures, would you run to Him for help?

Look at how Jesus gave a sinner the power to sin no more. He defended the woman who was caught in adultery. He looked tenderly into her eyes and asked her, "Woman, where are those accusers of yours? Has no one condemned you?" She said, "No one, Lord." And Jesus said to her, "Neither do I condemn you; go and sin no more." (John 8:10–11).

You see, the Ten Commandments, in all their pristine holiness, cannot make you holy and cannot put an end to sin. The power to stop sin from destroying your life comes from receiving the gift of **no condemnation** from Jesus. Your Savior, who has fulfilled the law on your behalf, says to you, "Where are those who condemn you? NEITHER DO I CONDEMN YOU. Now, go and sin no more." This is grace, my friend.

This is His unmerited favor! The law says that God will not condemn you only **if** you stop sinning. However, Grace says, "I have taken your condemnation on the cross. **Now**, you can go and sin no more."

Romans 6:14 says that **"sin shall not have dominion over you, for you are not under law but under grace [unmerited favor]."** If you are still struggling with sin, it is time to stop depending on the law. Fall upon His unmerited favor like the apostle Paul did. When you know that Christ has made you righteous apart from your works, and that He has perfected you by His unmerited favor, that will give you the ability to overcome every sinful temptation, habit and addiction in your life!

Right now, when you reach out to your Savior Jesus, God sees you as perfect in Him. He does not condemn you for your past, present and even future mistakes because all the mistakes that you will make in this life have already been nailed to the cross. You are now free to sin no more, experiencing victory and success over every sin and bondage in your life!

❖

Today's Prayer

Father, I thank You that I have the ability to overcome every sinful temptation, habit and addiction in my life because of Your abundant grace and gift of no condemnation. Thank You for showing me that it is Your grace, and not the law, that transforms me from inside out. Only by Your unmerited favor and not my efforts am I changed from glory to glory. I receive Your gift of no condemnation anew today and thank You for victory over every sin and bondage in my life.

Today's Thought
Knowing that Christ has made me righteous apart from my works
gives me the ability to overcome every sinful temptation,
habit and addiction in my life!

Today's Reflection On Favor

_____

_____

_____

_____

_____

_____

_____

_____

_____

_____

_____

_____

_____

_____

_____

_____

_____

_____

DAY 62

Continue In God's Grace

❖

Today's Scripture

*...Having begun in the Spirit, are you now being made
perfect by the flesh? —Galatians 3:3*

How were you first impacted by Jesus? Was it through the law or
was it His grace in your life that touched your heart? We all began our
relationship with the Lord because we were impacted by His love and
grace. Let us then continue in that grace.

**Don't start with grace and end up with the law. Don't start
with the new covenant, only to turn back to the old covenant!**

Paul warned the Galatians against turning back to the law after
beginning in grace. He said, "I marvel that you are turning away so soon
from Him who called you in the grace [unmerited favor] of Christ, to a
different gospel, which is not another; but there are some who trouble
you and want to **pervert the gospel of Christ**" (Galatians 1:6–7). Paul
takes this very seriously. He calls any gospel apart from the gospel of
grace (God's unmerited favor) a **perversion**. Attempting to be **justified**
by the works of the Ten Commandments is a perversion of the gospel
of Christ.

Paul asked the church in Galatia point-blank, "...Did you receive the
Spirit by the works of the law, or by the hearing of faith? Are you so
foolish? Having begun in the Spirit, are you now being made perfect by
the flesh [self-effort]?" (Galatians 3:2–3). Paul was saying to them, "You
began by believing in His grace, why are you now depending on your
works? That is foolishness! You should be continuing in His unmerited

favor!" These are strong words by Paul. Don't start with grace and end up with the law. Don't start with the new covenant, only to turn back to the old covenant! There are those who say that they are not justified by the law, but believe that they should keep the law for sanctification. My friend, both justification and sanctification come by our faith in Jesus' finished work alone.

When you are established in the new covenant of grace, you will experience a tremendous sense of confidence and security in Christ. When your confidence is in His unmerited favor and not your performance, you will not feel as if you are constantly jumping in and out of His favor and acceptance.

It is unfortunate that some believers have put themselves back under the old covenant without realizing it. Sometimes, they feel that God is on their side, but at other times, they feel that God is far away from them. Sometimes, they feel that God is satisfied with them, but at other times, they feel that God is angry with them. All these feelings are based predominantly on their own evaluation of how **they** have performed, how **they feel** about themselves, and not how God sees them. Because there is no new covenant scriptural basis for such evaluations, they end up arbitrarily deciding if they are deserving of God's blessings and favor in their lives or not, when in fact, they actually have access to His blessings all the time, simply because of Jesus and His finished work at the cross. Today, think, talk and act knowing that it is not about you or your works—it is about Jesus and Him alone, and step out into His blessings for you!

❖

Today's Prayer
Father, I thank You that it was Your grace that first impacted me and changed me forever. Help me to continue in that grace, always looking at Jesus and what He has done for me. I thank You that I am under the new covenant, which means that You are always on my side, and that Your presence and blessings are mine to enjoy.

Today's Thought
My focus will not be on me and what I have done,
but upon Jesus and what He has done.

Today's Reflection On Favor

_____

_____

_____

_____

_____

_____

_____

_____

_____

_____

_____

_____

_____

_____

_____

_____

_____

_____

_____

_____

God's Grace Transforms Us

❖

Today's Scripture

Since you are precious and honored in my sight, and because I love you...
—Isaiah 43:4 NIV

WOULD YOU AGREE with me that more Christians today know about the Ten Commandments than about the new covenant of God's unmerited favor? For that matter, if you walked down Times Square in New York City and started to interview people at random, most would probably have heard about the Ten Commandments, but know nothing about the new covenant of grace that came by Jesus Christ. In fact, the world identifies Christianity with the Ten Commandments. Isn't it sad that the world knows us by the laws that are obsolete and not by the unmerited favor that Christ died to give us?

When you catch a revelation of Jesus and just how precious you are in His sight, your life will be supernaturally transformed.

It is no wonder we are losing a whole new generation of young people to the world! The law holds no appeal or attraction and the Bible itself calls the law obsolete (Hebrews 8:13). If we keep on shoving the Ten Commandments down the throats of our young people, don't be surprised when they are turned off by legalistic forms of Christianity. More importantly, don't forget that the strength of sin is the law. The law has no power to stop sin. The law will not impart to them their precious identity in Christ, which will give them the strength to abstain from premarital sex, prevent them from getting into drug abuse and stop them from losing their sexual identity. Only God's own sacrifice on the cross can give them their new identity as a new creation in Christ Jesus!

Young people, when you catch a revelation of Jesus and just how precious you are in His sight, your lives will be supernaturally transformed. You will stop being harassed by suicidal thoughts. You will stop wanting to put yourselves at risk to "fit in" or to get the attention that you crave.

Young ladies, you will come to see and value yourselves differently as you learn to value yourselves in the same way Jesus values you. Overflowing with Jesus' perfect love for and acceptance of you, you will not be under the illusion that you need to give your bodies away to find acceptance and love from some guy. You will love yourselves as Jesus loves you!

Young men, you will develop supernatural self-control to manage your raging hormones. You will do it not by your own willpower, but through Jesus' power flowing through you. You will learn how to flee youthful lusts. You will know that being "cool" means respecting the opposite sex, and not putting yourselves and your girlfriends at risk of contracting sexually transmitted diseases and having unwanted pregnancies.

Young people, when you know that Jesus has an awesome destiny laid out for you, the desire to be involved in gangs and destructive activities such as alcohol and drug abuse and promiscuity will dissipate in Jesus' unmerited favor and love for you. Supernaturally, your desires for the things of the world will disappear as they get replaced with the desire for Jesus! That's the power of God's grace (unmerited favor) and His unconditional acceptance of us through the cross. What the law could not do, God did for us by sending His own Son Jesus Christ!

Today's Prayer

Father, I thank You that I am a new creation in Christ Jesus. All my sins have been forgiven. You remember them no more and see me righteous in Christ. I thank You that I am precious in Your sight, deeply loved by You, and that You have an awesome destiny for me!

Today's Thought

I am deeply loved by God, precious in His sight, with an awesome destiny to fulfill!

Today's Reflection On Favor

_____

_____

_____

_____

_____

_____

_____

_____

_____

_____

_____

_____

_____

_____

_____

_____

DAY 64

Transformed By God's Favor

❖

Today's Scripture

...the goodness of God leads you to repentance... —Romans 2:4

LET ME SHARE with you a testimony of a youth whose life has been wonderfully transformed by the unmerited favor of God. This young man smoked his first cigarette when he was only nine years old. By the time he was 14, he was already a seasoned gangster, peddling as well as taking drugs, and selling pirated movies.

Christianity is an intimate relationship with a loving God.

With the money earned, he would treat his gang members to fancy clothes or meals, and even cover transport expenses for them to congregate for gang fights! At 15, the law caught up with him and he was sent to a boys' reformatory home where he realized that his life needed to be turned around. And that was when God came into the picture. He said:

The home was where I first encountered God, even though I did not know it was Him then. One of my counselors, a Christian lady, prayed for me and for the first time in my life, I felt that there was "someone" watching over me. I did not think much about it then, but that's when my heart and my perspective on life began to change.

I started attending New Creation Church (NCC) in September 2005. A friend had invited me to NCC earlier, but I declined. However, one day I happened to oversleep on the train and missed my stop. The platform I got off on was completely deserted, but I noticed a plastic bag left on one of the benches. I looked at its contents to see if I could tell who it belonged to and realized that inside it were actually sermon CDs from NCC!

So even when I didn't want to attend NCC, God sent the church to me! It was no coincidence. It was God-directed! When I played the CDs at home out of curiosity, the presence of God was so real. I experienced such intimacy with God. As I listened to Pastor Prince's teachings, I knew that this was the God I had always believed in, **a God who loves me regardless of who I am or what I do***!*

Pastor Prince's teachings have set me free and given me a supernatural strength and passion to do His work. I don't feel any more bondage when it comes to communicating with God, knowing that He can lead me in every situation.

The most significant change I have experienced has been my inward transformation. I used to have a very bad temper, which got me into a lot of fights because I was easily provoked. **Being conscious of His love for me** *has delivered me from that. I also went from failing in high school to doing well enough in the polytechnic to qualify for a place in a university.*

This young man is now a confident, cheerful person with a bright future. He gives talks at schools and at the boys' reformatory home that he was in to share his journey with the youths and to encourage them. His life has been so incredibly transformed that even a government agency has enlisted him to speak to troubled youths. He says that ever since Jesus entered His life, he has seen His grace and favor superabound in his life. Many doors have opened for him and his life has really been enriched, with breakthroughs in areas such as his work, studies, family and relationships. Let's give Jesus all the glory!

That's what our young people need—a revelation of Jesus' perfect love for them! There is a lost and dying world out there. My friend, the Ten Commandments **cannot** be the only thing that youths know about Christianity anymore! How can they help but think that Christianity is nothing but rules, laws and regulations on what they should or should not be doing? How can they help but imagine God to be someone who is angry with them and looking for opportunities to punish them? If the young people in your community are to come to Jesus, they will need to know that Christianity is **an intimate relationship** with a loving God. Once they know this, they will be banging down the doors of churches every Sunday to get in to hear Jesus and His grace preached!

Beloved, I pray that like the young man whose testimony you just read, you will continue to allow Jesus to show you more and more of His perfect love for you every day.

Today's Prayer

Father, I thank You that You have not given me a code of rules to live by, but an intimate and loving relationship with You. I want to know You more and more each day. Show me more of Your love today, so that I may face every challenge with confidence and boldness.

Today's Thought

It is God's grace that is transforming my life.

Today's Reflection On Favor

_____

_____

_____

_____

_____

_____

_____

_____

_____

_____

_____

_____

_____

Whose Love Is Perfect?

❖

Today's Scripture

For God so loved the world that He gave His only begotten Son, that whoever believes in Him should not perish but have everlasting life.
—John 3:16

WHEN I WAS the president of my youth ministry, I used to preach hard and strong messages, telling my youths, "You've got to love God! You've got to love the Lord with all your heart, all your mind and all your soul!" All that time, when I was preaching this to the young people, I was wondering to myself, "How in the world do I do that?" I would look at myself and check my heart, mind and soul—did I really love the Lord that perfectly? How could I expect my youths to love the Lord that way when I knew that I myself had failed? At that time, I was not established in the new covenant of grace yet. I did not know that by preaching that way, I was actually placing all my youths under the law because the sum total of the law is to love God with all your heart, all your soul, all your mind and all your strength (Matthew 22:37–40, Mark 12:29–30).

When you are overflowing with God's love, you will fulfill the law effortlessly without even trying.

Let me ask you this: Has anybody ever been able to love the Lord with all his heart, mind and soul? No one. Not a single person has been able to do that. God knew all the while that under the law, no one could love Him that perfectly. So do you know what He did? The Bible says, "For God **so** loved the world that He gave His only begotten Son..." I love that little word "so." It speaks of the intensity with which God loves us.

When God sent Jesus, He was effectively saying this to us: "I know that you can't love Me perfectly, so watch Me now. **I** will love you with all My heart, all My soul, all My mind and all My strength." And He stretched His arms wide and died for us. This is what the Bible says about what Jesus did on the cross: "For scarcely for a righteous man will one die; yet perhaps for a good man someone would even dare to die. But God **demonstrates His own love toward us**, in that while we were still sinners, Christ died for us. Much more then, having now been justified by His blood, we shall be saved from wrath through Him" (Romans 5:7–9).

My friend, the cross is not a demonstration of our perfect love and devotion to God. The cross is God's demonstration of **His** perfect love and **His** perfect grace (unmerited favor) toward us, for it was while we were **still** sinners that Jesus died for us. He did not die for you and me because of our perfect love for God. He died for you and me because of HIS perfect love for us! Let me give you the Bible's definition of love to make this even clearer for you: "In this is love, **not that we loved God, but that He loved us** and sent His Son to be the propitiation for our sins" (1 John 4:10). Beloved, that's the emphasis of the new covenant of grace (unmerited favor)—HIS love for us, not our love for Him!

As we raise up a new generation of believers, let us raise up a generation that is impacted by God's unmerited favor and that boasts in His love for us. When we receive His love for us and start believing that we are His beloved, look at the result that 1 John 4:11 spells out: "Beloved, if God so loved us, we also ought to love one another." Notice that the love for one another comes after our experience of His love for us! It stems from an overflow. You cannot love others when you have not first been filled by His love. And when you are overflowing with His love, you will fulfill the law effortlessly without even trying because God's Word tells us, "Love does no harm to a neighbor; therefore **love is the fulfillment of the law**" (Romans 13:10). Step into that river today. Change the quality of your relationships by believing and being conscious of the fact that you are His beloved!

❖

Today's Prayer

*Father, I know that I can never love You perfectly with all my heart,
all my soul and all my strength. So I thank You that You love me
every day with all Your heart, all Your soul and all Your strength.
Whenever I see the cross, I see YOUR PERFECT love for me!
Fill me with a greater revelation of Your love for me till I am
overflowing with it and touching and impacting others.*

Today's Thought

*Loving others comes naturally when I know
that I am so loved by God.*

Today's Reflection On Favor

_____

_____

_____

_____

_____

_____

_____

_____

_____

_____

_____

_____

_____

_____

_____

_____

You Are An Heir Of The World!

❖

Today's Scripture

Christ has redeemed us from the curse of the law, having become a curse
for us (for it is written, "Cursed is everyone who hangs on a tree"), that
the blessing of Abraham might come upon the Gentiles in Christ Jesus,
that we might receive the promise of the Spirit through faith.
—Galatians 3:13–14

GOD'S BLESSINGS ARE part of our inheritance in the new covenant of grace, which Jesus died to give us. God's Word tells us that "Christ has redeemed us from the curse of the law, having become a curse for us... that **the blessing of Abraham** might come upon the Gentiles in Christ Jesus, that we might receive the promise of the Spirit through faith." Isn't it interesting that the Lord is very specific in mentioning that Christ became a curse for us on the cross, so that we can experience and enjoy the blessing of Abraham? He does not want us to simply experience any kind of blessing. He wants us to experience **the blessing of Abraham**. I think it behooves us then to find out what "the blessing of Abraham" is and who can receive it.

Every believer in Christ is an heir. "Heir" speaks of
an inheritance that is yours not because of what
you do, but because of whose you are.

The Bible tells us that "if you are Christ's, then you are Abraham's seed, and heirs according to the promise" (Galatians 3:29). Are you Christ's? Do you belong to Jesus? Then that makes you an heir **according to the promise**. Every believer in Christ is an heir. Whenever you hear the word "heir," it speaks of something good. It speaks of an inheritance that you don't work for, an inheritance that is yours not because of what you do, but because of **whose** you are. In this case, as a new covenant believer in Jesus, you belong to Jesus and you have a blood-bought inheritance in Christ as the seed of Abraham. You, beloved, are an heir according to THE promise!

Now, there are many promises in the Bible, but what is THE promise that God made to Abraham? We can't claim this promise if we don't know what it is. We need to go to the Word (use the Bible to interpret the Bible) to establish what the promise is. And we find the answer in Romans 4:13—"For **the promise** that he would be the **heir of the world** was not to Abraham or to his seed through the law, but through the righteousness of faith."

The promise to Abraham and his seed (you and I) is that he would be "the heir of the world"! In the original Greek text, the word "world" here is *kosmos*. Its meaning includes, "the whole circle of earthly goods, endowments, riches, advantages, pleasures."[1] Now, **that** is what you are an heir to through Jesus' finished work! In Christ, you are an heir of the world—its goods, its endowments, its riches, its advantages and its pleasures. This is THE promise that God made to Abraham and his seed. Don't apologize for it. It is your inheritance in Christ!

❖

Today's Prayer

Father, I thank You that I am an heir of the world because I am Abraham's seed through Christ. I have such a rich inheritance not because I have done anything to deserve it, but because Jesus qualified me through His death and resurrection. And since Jesus died to give me this wonderful inheritance, I will not apologize for it, but expect to experience and enjoy it!

Today's Thought

I am an heir of the world through Jesus' finished work!

Today's Reflection On Favor

_____

_____

_____

_____

_____

_____

_____

_____

_____

_____

_____

_____

_____

_____

_____

_____

_____

_____

_____

_____

Blessed To Be A Blessing

❖

Today's Scripture

I will make you a great nation; I will bless you and make your name great; and you shall be a blessing. —Genesis 12:2

WHAT DOES IT mean to be an heir of the world? Let's take a look at Abraham's life to see what the Lord did for him. God's Word tells us that Abraham did not just become rich. He became very rich.

The success that we, as new covenant believers, can believe God for is good, holistic success that permeates every aspect of our lives!

"Well, Pastor Prince, being an heir of the world refers to spiritual riches."

Hang on, that is not what my Bible says. According to Genesis 13:2, Abraham was "very rich in livestock, in silver, and in gold." Now, if financial blessings are not part of the blessings of the Lord, then are you telling me that the Lord cursed Abraham with wealth? I am so glad that God defined Abraham's riches very specifically. God must have foreseen a generation of people who would argue that He is against His people experiencing financial success, so He said clearly in His Word that Abraham was very rich in livestock, silver and gold. Abraham wasn't just rich spiritually. Beloved, God is not against you having wealth, but He is definitely against wealth having you.

The Lord blessed Abraham so that he could be a blessing to others. He told Abraham, "...I will bless you...and you shall be a blessing." Similarly, He will bless you financially, so that **you** can be a blessing to others. You cannot be a blessing to those around you—your loved ones, local church, community and the poor—if you are not blessed by the Lord first.

Now, you already know that finances alone don't make you a success. There are a lot of "poor" people in the world today who have a lot of money. They can have fat bank accounts, but their hearts are empty without the revelation of Jesus' love for them. You and I have something from Jesus that is far more superior. The success that we, as new covenant believers, can believe God for is good, holistic success that permeates every aspect of our lives!

What keeps you safe for financial success is when you know that your blessings come by Jesus' unmerited favor. When you have that revelation, you will no longer be preoccupied with having money because you will be preoccupied with the Lord. Amazingly, you will realize that the more occupied you are with Jesus, the more money follows after you! Now, why is that? It is simply because when you seek first the kingdom of God, and put Jesus, His righteousness (not your own righteousness), His joy and His peace as your first priority, God's Word promises you that ALL the material things that you need will be added to you (Matthew 6:33).

The Lord always gives you money with a mission and prosperity with a purpose. He blesses you and when you are blessed, you can be a vessel to bless others. The gospel of grace can be preached, churches can be built, precious lives can be touched, sinners can be born again, marriages can be restored and physical bodies can be healed when you send out the Word of Jesus with your financial support.

Don't love money and use people. Use money to love people. May it be settled in your heart once and for all that it is God's desire for you to be a financial success and to have more than enough to bless others!

❖

Today's Prayer

Father, I thank You that Your blessings for me include financial prosperity. I know that You are not against me having money, but You don't want the love of money to keep me in bondage. I ask that You prosper me financially, so that I may use money for Your kingdom work and to bless those in need. Keep me safe for financial success. Help me keep my eyes on Jesus—always preoccupied with Him and His purposes, and never forgetting that every blessing comes by Your unmerited favor.

Today's Thought

Don't love money and use people. Use money to love people.

Today's Reflection On Favor

_____

_____

_____

_____

_____

_____

_____

_____

_____

_____

_____

_____

_____

_____

_____

_____

_____

DAY 68

Your Blessings Include Health And Renewal Of Youth

❖

Today's Scripture

Who satisfies your mouth with good things, so that your youth is renewed like the eagle's. —Psalm 103:5

BEING AN HEIR of the world does not just mean having financial prosperity. Let's look at what else it means to be an heir of the world. What other blessings did Abraham receive? We know that Abraham was healthy and strong, and so was Sarah, his wife. The Lord renewed their youth so dramatically that when Abraham was about 100 years old and Sarah about 90, Sarah conceived Isaac after many years of barrenness.

You can trust the Lord to renew your youth as He did for Abraham and Sarah!

When God blesses, His blessings include fecundity, which is fruitfulness in childbearing. Nobody can argue that Abraham and Sarah's renewal of youth was merely spiritual. Isaac is proof that the renewal they experienced was physical as well. As an heir of the world, the Lord will likewise cause you to be strong and healthy. It is not possible to be an heir of the world if you are constantly fatigued, sick and flat on your back. No way! God will make you healthy and keep you in divine health in Jesus' name!

Some years ago, I asked the Lord why the Bible calls every female believer a daughter of Sarah (1 Peter 3:6). There were many other women of faith in the Bible, such as Ruth and Esther. So why didn't God choose to refer to female believers as daughters of Ruth or daughters of Esther?

The Lord then showed me in His Word that Sarah was the only woman in the Bible who had her youth renewed in her old age. We see evidence of Sarah's renewal of youth when she was pursued twice by two different kings who wanted to include her in their harems.

Do you know how old Sarah was when Pharaoh, the first of these kings, wanted her? She was about 65 years old! Now, if that is not evidence enough for you, do you know how old Sarah was when Abimelech, king of Gerar, wanted her? She was about 90 years old! Hey, these were *heathen* kings. I am sure that they were not captivated by her inner or spiritual beauty. Sarah must have had her physical youth renewed for these kings to desire her in her old age. Ladies, are you getting this? The Lord calls you daughters of Sarah. You can trust the Lord to renew your youth as He did for Sarah!

God's Word promises a renewal of your youth and strength. There are two passages in the Bible that I want you to read for yourself. Psalm 103:1–5 says:

> Bless the Lord, O my soul; and all that is within me, bless His holy name! Bless the Lord, O my soul, and forget not all His benefits: Who forgives all your iniquities, who heals all your diseases, who redeems your life from destruction, who crowns you with lovingkindness and tender mercies, who satisfies your mouth with good things, **so that your youth is renewed like the eagle's**.

Meanwhile, Isaiah 40:31 promises this:

> But those who wait on the Lord shall renew their strength; they shall mount up with wings like eagles, they shall run and not be weary, they shall walk and not faint.

As in Sarah's case, we can experience a literal renewal in our physical bodies. Let us believe God for this physical renewal of our youth, and that after this renewal, we will have a youthful body, but a wise and experienced mind. Now, that is a powerful combination and that's the kind of renewal that God wants to give us.

My friend, God wants you to be strong and healthy. It is not His plan for you to be sick. Sickness, viruses and diseases are not from Him, and He would certainly not put sickness on you to teach you a lesson, any more than you would put sickness on your children to teach them a lesson! Be very clear that God does not and will not discipline you with sicknesses, accidents and diseases. We are on the same side as doctors, fighting the same battle against sickness.

Beloved, it is very important for you to get this doctrine right so that you can believe right. What hope is there and how can you have a confident expectation to be healed if you erroneously think that your condition is from the Lord? It is time for you to stop being deceived by wrong teachings. Just look at the ministry of Jesus to see God's heart for you. Look at the four Gospels. What happened every time Jesus came in contact with a sick person? The sick person got healed! You will never find Jesus going up to a perfectly healthy person and saying, "I want to teach you a lesson on humility and patience. Now, receive some leprosy!" No way! Yet, that is basically what some people are saying about our Lord today.

Now, tell me, what happened each time Jesus saw lack? When the little boy brought his five loaves and two fish to Jesus, did He gobble them up and say, "I am giving you a lesson about poverty"? Of course not! Jesus took the five loaves and two fish, multiplied them and fed more than 5,000 people with 12 baskets full of leftovers (John 6:8–13)! That's my Jesus! He did not feed the multitudes with just enough food. He blessed them with more than enough food. He is the God of more than enough and that is His style. Likewise, Jesus wants to bless you with more than enough, so that you can be a blessing to others!

❖

Today's Prayer

Father, thank You for all the blessings of provision, health, strength and renewal of youth which I can experience because of Jesus' finished work at the cross. Today, as I look to You and wait upon You, renew my youth and strength, so that I may mount up with wings like eagles. I want to run and not be weary, walk and not faint. Grant me good health all the days of my life. I want to glorify You in my body, enjoy all that You have blessed me with and be able to fulfill all Your plans and purposes for me!

Today's Thought

What God did for Abraham and Sarah—renewal of youth—
God can do for me too!

Today's Reflection On Favor

_____

_____

_____

_____

_____

_____

_____

_____

_____

_____

_____

_____

_____

_____

DAY 69

Nearness To God And Protection In The Beloved

❖

Today's Scripture

You shall dwell in the land of Goshen, and you shall be near to me, you and your children, your children's children, your flocks and your herds, and all that you have. There I will provide for you, lest you and your household, and all that you have, come to poverty; for there are still five years of famine. —Genesis 45:10–11

In the Old Testament story of Joseph, after Joseph revealed himself to his brothers, he tells them to return to their father and to tell him, "... come down to me, do not tarry. You shall dwell in the land of **Goshen**, and you shall be **near to me**, you and your children, your children's children, your flocks and your herds, and all that you have." (Genesis 45:9–10) The name "Goshen" means "drawing near."[1] God wants you to be in "Goshen," which is a place of nearness to Him, and there is no place nearer to Him than being in the Beloved. God's heart of love is not satisfied with just removing your sins from you. No, He wants more. He wants you in His presence. He wants you in the place where He can lavish the bountiful love in His heart on you!

Remember that as God's beloved child, you are in the world, but not of the world.

When you draw near to Jesus, look what happens. Joseph tells his brothers to also tell their father, **"There I will provide for you,** lest you and your household, and all that you have, come to poverty; for there are still five years of famine." When you draw near to your heavenly Joseph, He will provide for you and your little ones. In the midst of financial famine in the world, in the midst of rising fuel and food costs, do not despair. Draw near to Jesus, for there in "Goshen," in that place of nearness, He will provide for you and your household. Your God shall supply ALL your needs according to HIS riches (not according to your bank account balance or to the world's economic situation) in glory by Christ Jesus (Philippians 4:19)!

That's not all, my friend. Another blessing that you can enjoy when you are in the Beloved is divine protection. In recent years, new strains of deadly viruses have been making headlines. But whatever the virus may be, whether it's the bird flu or swine flu or some other new plague, you can safely claim Psalm 91 for yourself. You can declare, "A thousand may fall at my side, and ten thousand at my right hand; but it shall **not** come near me, God's beloved!" (Psalm 91:7).

When there were plagues and pestilences all over Egypt because Pharaoh refused to let God's people go, look at what God said about the children of Israel: "...I will **set apart** the land of Goshen, in which My people dwell, that no swarms of flies shall be there, in order that you may know that I am the Lord in the midst of the land. I will **make a difference** between My people and your people..." (Exodus 8:22–23). There is a difference between God's beloved people and the people of the world. Although Egypt was plagued by swarms of flies and other pestilences, the children of Israel were safe in the land of Goshen, completely untouched by the troubles!

So even if there are bad things happening in the world today, remember that as God's beloved child, you are **in** the world, but not **of** the world (John 17:11, 16). No plague, no evil and no danger can come close to you and your dwelling place because you are safe in the secret place of the Most High. As the children of Israel were kept safe and protected in Goshen, so will you and I, whom God calls His beloved!

Today's Prayer

Father, I thank You that You protect, deliver and provide for my family and me because I am in Christ Your Beloved. I thank You for Jesus and Your unmerited favor, and for making a difference between Your people and the people of the world. Today, as I go about my activities, I will fear no evil because I am Your beloved child enjoying divine protection and provision!

Today's Thought

*I am different from the people of the world—
I have a God who looks after me!*

Today's Reflection On Favor

_____

_____

_____

_____

_____

_____

_____

_____

_____

_____

_____

_____

_____

_____

_____

_____

Fear Robs You Of Your Inheritance In Christ

❖

Today's Scripture

Fear not, for I am with you; be not dismayed, for I am your God.
I will strengthen you, yes, I will help you, I will uphold you
with My righteous right hand. —Isaiah 41:10

LET'S LOOK AT Joshua 1, which records a critical point in Israel's history, to see what we can learn about having the "good success" that God promised Joshua. Joshua was appointed as the new leader of Israel after Moses died and he was to bring God's people into the Promised Land. This was a mammoth responsibility. Forty years before that, the children of Israel were on the brink of entering the Promised Land. But because they had refused to believe God's promises to them, that generation spent 40 years wandering in the wilderness.

We do not have to strive and strain to be blessed.
Good success for us today is enjoying the fruits
and labor of Another—Jesus Christ.

That was not God's will for them. God wanted to bring them into a land that was **flowing** with milk and honey. He wanted to give them a land filled with large and beautiful cities they did not build, houses full of good things they did not fill, hewn-out wells they did not dig, and vineyards and olive trees they did not plant (Deuteronomy 6:10–11). In other words, He wanted them to enjoy the fruits and labor of another—the giants who were in the land.

Beloved, *that* is good success. That's the kind of success where you enjoy abundance of provision in every area of your life. That kind of success that is characterized by rest because today, the Bible says that our promised land is God's rest (Hebrews 3:11). We are enjoying the fruits and labor of Another—Jesus Christ. And that's the kind of success Christ has given us today. We do not have to strive and strain to be blessed.

What caused the entire generation to be robbed of their promised inheritance? To answer this question, we need to ask another: Who were the leaders over that generation? The Lord showed me that Moses had followed his father-in-law's advice to appoint "able men, such as fear God, men of truth, hating covetousness" (Exodus 18:21) as his leaders to help him rule over the children of Israel.

The 12 spies who were sent to spy on Canaan must have been picked from this pool of leaders. This means that they were all able men who **feared God**, men of truth, hating covetousness. [By the way, when Jesus was tempted by the devil in the wilderness, He said, "Away with you, Satan! For it is written, 'You shall **worship** the Lord your God, and Him only you shall serve'" (Matthew 4:10). Jesus was quoting from Deuteronomy 6:13, which actually reads, "You shall **fear** the Lord your God and serve Him..." Jesus substituted the word "fear" with the word "worship." So according to Jesus, **to fear God is to worship God.**] But despite having all these leadership attributes, **none** of these spies or leaders whom Moses appointed entered the Promised Land apart from Joshua and Caleb. None! Why was this so?

The answer is this: They lacked courage! We can read an account of this story in Numbers 13:17–14:9. Moses sent 12 spies into the Promised Land. Only Joshua and Caleb came back with a good report of the land, saying, "The land we passed through to spy out is an exceedingly good land. If the Lord delights in us, then He will bring us into this land and give it to us, 'a land which flows with milk and honey.' Only do not rebel against the Lord, nor fear the people of the land, for they are our bread; their protection has departed from them, and the Lord is with us. Do not fear them" (Numbers 14:7–9). The other 10 spies gave a bad report, saying, "We are not able to go up against the people, for they are stronger than we...all the people whom we saw in it are men of great stature. There we saw the giants...and we were like grasshoppers in our own sight, and so we were in their sight" (Numbers 13:31–33).

They all saw the same land, the same giants, but what a stark contrast in the reports that they brought back! Joshua and Caleb had a different spirit (a spirit of faith, Numbers 14:24) and focused on the promises and goodness of God. But the rest cowered in fear and saw only the giants and challenges in the land. They had good leadership qualities, but it was all negated because they were **fearful**. Fear paralyzed them! The nation of Israel could only go as far as their leaders could bring them. Because their leaders were fearful, the entire generation was robbed of God's promises for their lives!

Today, no matter how dire your circumstances may appear, choose to focus on the goodness of God. Choose to see how Christ has paid the price for you to enjoy God's unmerited favor, peace, protection and provision in every area of your life. Fear will not paralyze you. Instead, you will see His faithfulness and walk in all His blessings!

❖

Today's Prayer

Father, strengthen me today and uphold me with Your righteous right hand. Give me a greater sense of Your abiding presence, so that I will not fear, but be able to face all my challenges today with boldness and courage, knowing that You are my help, my wisdom and my strength. All I need to do is walk in the victory that Jesus has already won for me.

Today's Thought

I won't be afraid for God Almighty is with me!

Today's Reflection On Favor

_____

_____

_____

_____

_____

_____

_____

_____

_____

_____

_____

_____

_____

_____

_____

_____

_____

_____

As Jesus Is Today, So Are You!

❖

Today's Scripture

*Love has been perfected among us in this: that we may have boldness
in the day of judgment; because as He is, so are we in this world.*
—*1 John 4:17*

IT IS WONDERFUL to know that God does not measure and judge you
based on your performance today. Instead, He looks at Jesus, and as
Jesus is, that is how He sees you. His Word declares that "love has been
perfected among us in this: that we may have boldness in the day of
judgment; because **as He is, so are we in this world.**"

**As new covenant believers, we do not have to fear the day of
judgment simply because all our sins have been completely
judged at the cross, and as Jesus is, so are we!**

As new covenant believers, we do not have to fear the day of
judgment simply because all our sins have been completely judged
at the cross, and as Jesus is, so are we! Notice that it does not say
that "as Jesus was on earth, so are we in this world." That would have
been amazing enough because during Jesus' ministry on earth, healing,
blessings and abundance followed Him everywhere He went. Yet, that
is not what the Word says. What it says is, "as Jesus **is**" (notice the use
of the present tense). In other words, as He is **right now**, so are we in
this world.

What a powerful revelation! Just consider where Jesus is today. The
Bible tells us:

...He [God] raised Him [Jesus] from the dead and **seated Him at His right hand** in the heavenly places, far above all principality and power and might and dominion, and every name that is named, not only in this age but also in that which is to come. And He put all things under His feet, and gave Him to be head over all things to the church, which is His body, the fullness of Him who fills all in all.

—Ephesians 1:20–23

Jesus is seated at the Father's right hand today, in a position of power and authority. If I were you, I would take some time to meditate on this passage because the Bible tells us that as Jesus is, so are we right now, in this world. Meditate on how as Jesus is "far above all principality and power and might and dominion, and every name that is named," so are we! See it in God's Word for yourself. See yourself as Jesus is, far above every principality and power, far above every disease and physical condition, far above every kind of fear, depression and addiction, and begin to reign over every negative situation in your life today!

❖

Today's Prayer

Father, I thank You for placing me in the best position there is in the universe—in Christ at Your right hand in heavenly places! Therefore, I am far above all principality and power and might and dominion, and every name that is named, not only in this age, but also in the age to come! As Jesus is healthy, wise, victorious and successful today, so am I right now in this world!

Today's Thought

*I am seated with Christ at the Father's right hand,
far above every known or unknown problem!*

Today's Reflection On Favor

_____

_____

_____

_____

_____

_____

_____

_____

_____

_____

_____

_____

_____

_____

_____

_____

_____

_____

_____

_____

Trust God, Not Man Or Self-Effort

❖

Today's Scripture

…Cursed is the man who trusts in man and makes flesh his strength…
—Jeremiah 17:5

Today I want to show you the difference between a blessed man and a cursed man. The Bible is amazingly clear on how you can be a cursed man and what a cursed life looks like. God's Word also shows you a picture of a blessed man and how you can be that man.

Let's start with how one can be a cursed man. Jeremiah 17:5 tells us that when a man "trusts in man" and not in the Lord, he becomes a cursed man. To trust in man also refers to someone putting confidence in his own good works and efforts, claiming to be "self-made," choosing to depend on himself and rejecting God's unmerited favor.

We can never bring about good success that comes from God by depending on our self-efforts.

A man who "makes flesh his strength" is also cursed. When you see the word "flesh" in your Bible, it does not always refer to your physical body. You have to look at the context of the verse. In this context, "flesh" can be paraphrased as "self-effort." In other words, we can read verse five as "Cursed is the man who trusts in man and makes **self-effort** his strength."

My friend, there are essentially two ways to live this life. The first is for us to depend and trust entirely in the Lord's unmerited favor, while the other is to depend on our efforts, and strive and struggle for success. We can never bring about good success that comes from God by depending on our self-efforts. No matter how we strive and struggle, we cannot work for our own righteousness or attain our own forgiveness. Any success that we may achieve is only partial success.

On the other hand, God's kind of success is complete, whole and permeates into every facet of our lives—spirit, soul and body. God's Word says, "The blessing of the Lord makes one rich, and He adds no sorrow with it" (Proverbs 10:22). God never gives us success at the expense of our marriage, families or health. Like I always say to the business people in my church, don't use all your health to chase after wealth, only to spend all your wealth later to get your health back! Which man is enjoying greater prosperity? A man who has a fat bank account but is flat on his back with sickness, or one who may not have much in his bank account but is enjoying divine health?

Look around you. It is clear that true prosperity and good success cannot be measured in terms of how much money we have in our bank accounts. With the unmerited favor of God, the man who may not have much at this point in his life **will** experience good success.

Health and wholeness in your physical body are part of God's blessings. If you are constantly under tremendous stress and have regular panic attacks because of the nature of your work, then I would encourage you to take a step back and seek the Lord's counsel. Stress robs you of health, whereas good success from the Lord causes your youth to be renewed.

When you depend on your efforts, you can struggle for many years and get only a certain measure of success. But God's ways are higher. With just one moment of His favor, you can experience accelerated blessings and promotion that years of striving and struggling can never achieve.

Look at Joseph's life. He was nothing but a lowly prisoner. Yet, within an hour of meeting Pharaoh, he was promoted to the highest office in the entire Egyptian empire. Beloved, even if you are down and out (like Joseph was) at this point in your life, the Lord can promote you supernaturally in an instant when you choose to put your eyes on Him!

Today's Prayer

Father, I don't want to put my trust in man or my self-efforts. I choose to put my trust in You and Your unmerited favor. Help me to depend on and see Your goodness and grace toward me every day, so that I can experience Your good success without the stress. I thank You that one moment of Your unmerited favor can cause me to experience accelerated blessings and promotion that years of striving and struggling can never achieve.

Today's Thought

One moment of God's favor yields far more than years of hard, stressful labor.

Today's Reflection On Favor

_____

_____

_____

_____

_____

_____

_____

_____

_____

_____

_____

_____

A Man Under Grace Sees And Appreciates His Blessings

❖

Today's Scripture

...Cursed is the man who trusts in man and makes flesh his strength...
For he shall be like a shrub in the desert, and shall not
see when good comes... —Jeremiah 17:5–6

ONE OF THE saddest things about a man who trusts in his strengths
and self-efforts—"who...makes flesh his strength"—is that he cannot
see good when it comes his way.

As a pastor, I have seen, down through the years, people who don't
put their trust in the Lord when it comes to their marriages, finances
and other areas of weakness. They are determined to trust in their own
efforts, and tend to be rather arrogant and frustrated with the people
around them. Many a time, when you observe people like that, you
realize that they cannot see the good things that are right under their
noses. They don't appreciate their spouses, neglect their children and
even when other blessings come their way, **they miss them!**

People living under grace can truly enjoy the blessings
around them because they know that these
blessings are undeserved!

Why is it that they can't see good when it comes? It is because
people who trust in their own efforts have **no ability** to see and receive
blessings from the Lord. They only believe in the "good" that can come
from their own efforts. That is why they are proud. You would probably
notice that such people don't say "thank you" very often to the people

around them. They feel like they are entitled to and deserve whatever they receive. They are rarely grateful or appreciative, and that is why they take their spouses for granted instead of seeing them as a blessing from the Lord.

In contrast, people who are living under grace and who trust in the Lord's unmerited favor are constantly thankful, praising God and giving thanks to Jesus. They are grateful and appreciative of the people around them.

When I was still a bachelor, I had an idea of the kind of wife I wanted and brought my request to the Lord. But you know what? He over-answered my prayer and gave me Wendy! I am truly grateful to the Lord for Wendy and I know that it is the unmerited favor of Jesus. When I look at my daughter Jessica, I know that I don't deserve such a beautiful daughter, and yet the Lord gave this precious girl to me. You see, my friend, I did nothing to deserve it, but the Lord blessed me with an amazing family. When you live under grace, you can truly enjoy the blessings around you because you know that they are undeserved. Look at the family, friends and other blessings that God has given you today. See how He has blessed you with them because He loves you. And when you see them as blessings, they will enrich your life (Proverbs 10:22)!

❖

Today's Prayer

Father, I thank You that I am under Your unmerited favor. When You send blessings my way, I will see, appreciate and enjoy them. I know that I don't deserve any blessing from You, but You bless me nonetheless, because You love me and because of what Jesus has done for me at the cross. Father, for all that You have and are going to bless me with, I give You thanks, praise and glory.

Today's Thought

Every blessing in my life has come because of God's unmerited favor on me—how can I not be thankful for what I have!

Today's Reflection On Favor

_____

_____

_____

_____

_____

_____

_____

_____

_____

_____

_____

_____

_____

_____

_____

_____

_____

_____

_____

_____

_____

DAY 74

A Picture Of A Blessed Man

❖

Today's Scripture

Blessed is the man who trusts in the Lord, and whose hope is the Lord.
For he shall be like a tree planted by the waters, which spreads out
its roots by the river, and will not fear when heat comes; but its leaf
will be green, and will not be anxious in the year of drought,
nor will cease from yielding fruit. —Jeremiah 17:7–8

LET'S LOOK AT some of the pictures that the Bible paints for us in
Jeremiah 17. God's Word is amazing. He speaks to us through word
pictures and imagery in the Bible. For example, Jeremiah 17:5–6 paints
us a picture of a cursed man—"a shrub in the desert." What a dismal
image of a man! A person who is always trusting in himself is like a
dried-up shrub, looking old, tired and haggard.

The blessed man is not conscious of seasons of heat,
but continues to be strong and to flourish.

But thank God the Bible didn't just stop with the description of the
cursed man. It goes on to paint a beautiful picture of a blessed man:
"Blessed is the man who trusts in the Lord, and whose hope is the Lord.
For he shall be like a tree planted by the waters, which spreads out its
roots by the river, and will not fear when heat comes; but its leaf will
be green, and will not be anxious in the year of drought, nor will cease
from yielding fruit." Wow! I know which man I would rather be. Truly, a
picture is worth more than a thousand words! I want you to see yourself
as this tree planted by the waters today!

When I was on vacation with Wendy in the breathtaking Canadian
Rockies, we spent a lot of time just roaming around and soaking in the

splendor of our heavenly Father's creation. As we wandered along the bank of a tranquil river that we chanced upon, we found a majestic tree anchored by the water's edge. Its trunk was sturdy and strong, and its branches stretched out to form a perfect canopy above it. In contrast to the other trees that were further away from the river, its leaves were refreshingly green and luscious. This was because the tree was constantly nourished by the river.

Looking at that impressive, beautiful tree, I couldn't help but recall the blessed man described in Jeremiah 17, and I remember saying to myself then, "I am like this tree in Jesus' name!" When you depend on and trust in the Lord, you are like this tree too. Jesus will cause you to be a picture of robust strength, vitality and good success. See yourself like a beautiful tree planted by the waters. God's Word says that even when heat comes, you will not fear it!

Did you notice a crucial difference between the blessed man and the cursed man? While the cursed man cannot see good when it comes (Jeremiah 17:6), the blessed man will not fear even when heat comes! The King James Version says that the blessed man "shall **not see** when heat cometh." This is amazing. It means that heat comes even to the blessed man, but he is not conscious of seasons of heat, but continues to be strong and to flourish. He will be like a tree whose leaf continues to be green. When you are like the blessed man, you will be evergreen! This means that you will enjoy divine health, youthfulness, vitality and dynamism.

When you are blessed, your body will be full of life as the Lord renews your youth and vigor. Your health will not fail you, nor will you lose your youth. There will be no stress, fear and panic attacks because the blessed man "will not be anxious in the year of drought." A year of drought speaks of a severe famine, and in our modern vernacular, it would be no different from the global financial meltdown, the subprime crisis, the collapse of global investment banks, the volatile stock markets and rising inflation. While it may be bad news for the world, the blessed man can remain at rest and not be anxious because God has promised that even in the midst of a crisis, he will not "cease from yielding fruit." Beloved, be the blessed man who puts his trust in the Lord and this will also happen to you!

Today's Prayer

Father, because of Your unconditional love and grace toward me, I am a blessed man who is like an evergreen tree planted by the waters. I thank You that when the heat is on, I will not be fearful or anxious. I will not even notice it because I am covered by Your favor and lovingkindness. Indeed, Father, You will protect me, provide for me, keep me strong and healthy, and cause me to remain fruitful!

Today's Thought

I am like the tree planted by the waters— thriving, strong and fruitful!

Today's Reflection On Favor

_____

_____

_____

_____

_____

_____

_____

_____

_____

Right Place, Right Time

❖

Today's Scripture

...the race is not to the swift, nor the battle to the strong, nor bread to the
wise, nor riches to men of understanding, nor favor to men of skill;
but time and chance happen to them all. —*Ecclesiastes 9:11*

BELOVED, NEVER FORGET that "the race is not to the swift, nor the battle
to the strong...but **time and chance happen to them all**." God wants
you to have the right timing—His timing, and nothing is left to chance
because you are God's child. Psalm 37:23 says, "The steps of a good
man are ordered by the Lord." You are that "good man" because you
are the righteousness of God in Christ.

**Depend on God to cause you to be at the right place at the
right time, to have right happenings happen in your life!**

Now, look at the word "happen." In the original Hebrew text, it
is the word *qarah*, which means "to encounter, to meet (without pre-
arrangement), to chance to be present."[1] In a nutshell, it means "right
happening." My friend, you can depend on God to cause you to be at
the right place at the right time, to have right happenings happen in your
life! I am sure that you would agree that being at the right place at the
right time is a tremendous blessing. You certainly don't want to be at
the wrong place at the wrong time. That can lead to disastrous results.

But even if you think that you are at the wrong place at the wrong
time, such as when you are caught in a traffic jam or when you miss your
train, don't be too agitated. A delay can turn out to be God's protection
from an accident ahead. Sometimes, a delay of just a few seconds can
mean the difference between life and death!

In 2001, a brother in my church wrote in to share that his son's office was in the twin towers in New York. On one particular morning, his son's alarm clock did not go off and he ended up missing his regular train to work, and was late arriving at work. Had he been on time that morning, he would have been in his office when the planes plowed into the building during the devastating terrorist attacks on September 11.

In 2003, another brother from my church was in Jakarta, Indonesia, for a business trip. He was staying at the Marriott Hotel and he was in the lobby when a bomb went off just outside the hotel. The bomb tore through the lobby and he saw a body flying past him as the deafening blast reverberated all around him.

After the dust had settled, he found blood spattered on him and debris strewn all around, but amazingly, he was completely unhurt. At the very moment when the bomb exploded, he **happened** to walk behind a pillar and it protected him from the impact of the blast. Just think what would have happened to him if he had reached that pillar just a few seconds before or after the bomb went off!

No matter how intelligent you are, how fat your savings account is or how prestigious your family name may be, there is no way you can know beforehand when to position yourself behind a pillar just as a bomb that you are unaware of explodes near you. Only God can put you at the right place at the right time. It was the Lord who placed this brother behind the pillar at the precise moment. His steps were literally ordered by the Lord. All glory to Him! Jesus is our true pillar of protection!

God's faithfulness in protecting His beloved by putting them at the right place at the right time was demonstrated even more recently. Two massive explosions rocked Jakarta, Indonesia, again on the morning of July 17, 2009, and this time both the Marriott and the Ritz-Carlton hotels were the targets of terrorist attacks.

A lady from our church was in the lobby of the Ritz-Carlton when one of the bombs was detonated in the nearby restaurant where guests were having breakfast. The force of the explosion sent glass shards flying past her, ripping into the flesh of other guests who were standing in front of her. Amazingly, she was completely unharmed!

She shared that she had initially planned to have breakfast at that very restaurant at the time the bomb exploded. That would certainly have put her at the wrong place at the wrong time. If she had done so, she could have been killed by the blast in the restaurant. However, she shared that the reason she missed her usual breakfast time that morning was that she was caught up in reading a few devotional entries from my *Destined To Reign Devotional* and spending time with the Lord in her hotel room. The "delay" she experienced in reading my book kept her away from the restaurant and saved her life! Praise Jesus!

My friend, nothing happens by chance—the Lord knows how to place you at the right place and the right time! You can depend on Jesus for right happenings. They all come by His unmerited favor. In the new covenant of grace, the Bible says that the Lord Himself writes His laws on your heart (Hebrews 8:10). He can speak to you and guide you in everything that you do. Allow Him to lead you supernaturally!

❖

Today's Prayer

Father, I thank You that my steps are ordered by You because I am righteous in Christ. And because there is no detail of my plans or my life that escapes Your attention, I can trust You to position me at the right place at the right time, safe from any danger and set up for good success. Father, I look to You and Your unmerited favor to protect me and my family from all harm and make our way prosperous.

Today's Thought

*My steps are ordered by the Lord because
I am righteous in Him.*

Today's Reflection On Favor

_____

_____

_____

_____

_____

_____

_____

_____

_____

_____

_____

_____

_____

_____

_____

_____

_____

_____

Pray For *Qarah* Today

❖

Today's Scripture

*Then he said, "O Lord God of my master Abraham, please give me
success this day, and show kindness to my master Abraham."*
—Genesis 24:12

Bᴇʟᴏᴠᴇᴅ, I ᴡᴀɴᴛ to show you how you can pray for and experience
God's divine positioning for good success today.

There is a principle in interpreting God's Word known as "the
principle of first mention." Every time a word is mentioned for the first
time in the Bible, there is usually a special significance and lesson that
we can learn. Let's take a look at the first occurrence of the word *qarah*.[1]
It is found in Genesis 24, when Abraham sent his unnamed servant[2] to
look for a bride for Isaac, his son.

We need the Lord to give us *qarah* every day.

The unnamed servant arrived at a well outside the city of Nahor in the
evening and decided to stop there. There were so many young women
gathered to draw water there that he did not know who would be the
right woman for Isaac. So the unnamed servant prayed this prayer: "O
Lord God of my master Abraham, please give me **success** this day, and
show kindness to my master Abraham."

The word "success" here is the Hebrew word *qarah*, and this is the
first time it appears in the Bible. The servant essentially prayed, "Give
me *qarah* this day." It goes without saying that with the Lord's *qarah* or
positioning for right happenings, the servant found a beautiful virtuous
woman named Rebekah, who became Isaac's bride.

We need the Lord to give us *qarah* every day. I encourage you to pray the prayer of that unnamed servant. Tell the Lord, "Give me success—*qarah*—this day," and depend on His unmerited favor to cause you to be at the right place at the right time!

Today's Prayer

Father, show me kindness and give me qarah—*success—today.*
In whatever assignments, appointments or errands I have to
attend to today, I ask that You direct my steps and place me at
the right place at the right time, so that I can accomplish all that
I need to do with ease and experience Your good success.

Today's Thought

Success in my endeavors depends on the Lord who
positions me at the right place at the right time.

Today's Reflection On Favor

_____

_____

_____

_____

_____

_____

_____

_____

_____

_____

_____

Have Confidence In
The Unmerited Favor Of Jesus

❖

Today's Scripture

*And she went, and came, and gleaned in the field after the reapers: and
her hap was to light on a part of the field belonging unto Boaz,
who was of the kindred of Elimelech.* —Ruth 2:3 KJV

THERE IS A beautiful story of a Moabite woman named Ruth in the
Bible. In the natural, Ruth had everything against her. She was a poor
widow, and she was a Moabitess, a Gentile in the Jewish nation of Israel.
But even after her husband died, Ruth remained with her mother-in-law
Naomi. She left her family to follow Naomi back to Bethlehem, and
made Naomi's God—the God of Abraham, Isaac and Jacob—her God.

**Have confidence in the unmerited favor of Jesus and
He will cause you to be positioned at the right
place at the right time to experience success.**

Now, because of their poverty, Naomi and Ruth could not afford
to buy grain, and Ruth had to go out to the field to perform the menial
task of gleaning whatever the reapers had left behind. I want you to
notice that Ruth was depending on the Lord's favor for she said to
Naomi, "Please let me go to the field, and glean heads of grain after him
in whose sight I may find **favor**" (Ruth 2:2). Ruth was confident that
God would give her favor even though she was a foreigner and had no
connections with anyone in the field. She didn't even know whose part
of the field she would be able to glean in.

Look at the Bible's account of what happened next: "And she went,
and came, and gleaned in the field after the reapers: and her **hap** was

to light on a part of the field belonging unto Boaz, who was of the kindred of Elimelech." Of all the spots in the field that Ruth could have wandered into, her "**hap**" was to come to the part of the field that belonged to Boaz, who was a man of great wealth, and who also **happened** to be Naomi's relative. "Hap" is an old English word and it means "to happen" to be at the right place. However, in the original Hebrew text, the root of this word is the word *qarah*!

When Ruth trusted in God's unmerited favor, she *qarah*-ed or happened to come to the part of the field that belonged to Boaz. To cut a long story short, Boaz saw Ruth, fell in love with her and married her. Ruth was possibly at the lowest point of her life just before she met Boaz. All the natural factors were against her. But because she put her trust in the Lord, who put her at the right place at the right time, her situation was turned around completely. In fact, she became one of the few woman to be mentioned in the genealogy of Jesus in Matthew 1:5, which states that "Boaz begot Obed by Ruth." What an honor to be included in the genealogy of Jesus Christ. Talk about being at the right place at the right time!

My friend, no matter what natural circumstances may be against you today, have confidence in the unmerited favor of Jesus and He will give you what I call "*qarah* success." He will cause you to be positioned at the right place at the right time to experience His protection and success in your relationships, career and finances.

❖

Today's Prayer

Father, thank You for Your unmerited favor and for blessing me with qarah *moments. Because of Your favor, I know that any weakness, disqualification or lack that I may have in the natural will not prevent me from being positioned at the right place at the right time to experience Your blessings. I choose to lean on Your unmerited favor and I ask You to bless me with right happenings today. Thank You for turning around the negative situations in my life and giving me* qarah *success.*

Today's Thought
I will trust in the Lord's unmerited favor and
experience right happenings!

Today's Reflection On Favor

_____

_____

_____

_____

_____

_____

_____

_____

_____

_____

_____

_____

_____

_____

_____

_____

_____

Worldly Wisdom Versus God's Wisdom

❖

Today's Scripture

Blessed is the man who walks not in the counsel of the ungodly…
—*Psalm 1:1*

Today, I want to talk about how you can depend on God's wisdom to succeed. Wisdom from the Lord comes by God's unmerited favor. It is not something that you can study for or acquire with your efforts. Wisdom from the Lord is something that the world cannot have. This is not to say that the world does not have wisdom. Step into any bookstore today and you will find shelves full of books containing experts' theories and methods on all sorts of subjects. The majority of these, however, stem from **human wisdom**, which strengthens and builds up only the flesh.

What we need is not more "self-help."
What we need is the Lord's help!

Whether they know it or not, the people of the world are crying out for true wisdom from the Lord. Just look at the constant demand for self-help books. But what we need is not more "self-help." What we need is the Lord's help! Read books that are written by Spirit-filled believers and Christian leaders who encourage you to look to Jesus and not to yourself.

Psalm 1:1 tells us this from the start: "Blessed is the man who walks not in the counsel of the ungodly." Beloved, this means that there *is* counsel in human wisdom. But the man who does *not* walk according to the wisdom of the world is the man who is blessed. At the same time, if his delight is in Jesus, and he meditates on Jesus day and night, Psalm 1:3

says, "He shall be like a tree planted by the rivers of water, that brings forth its fruit in its season, whose leaf also shall not wither; and whatever he does shall prosper."

My friend, make a decision to walk in the counsel of the godly and not in the counsel of the world, and you will see whatever you do prosper. God has raised up men and women who are established in the truths of the new covenant, and who will help you keep your eyes on Jesus. In Him, you will find all the wisdom that pertains to life. The Bible tells us that in Him "are hidden all the treasures of wisdom and knowledge" (Colossians 2:2–3) for your success. Keep looking to Jesus, draw on His divine wisdom and see the difference it will make to you!

❖

Today's Prayer

Father, I make a decision today to walk in the counsel of the godly and not the ungodly. I want to live life according to Your wisdom and not the world's wisdom. I want to walk more and more in Your wisdom in every area of my life. Help me to keep my eyes on Jesus, in whom is hidden all the treasures of wisdom and knowledge. I know that as I meditate on Jesus and His grace, I shall be like a tree planted by the rivers of water—always fruitful and prospering in all that I do. Thank You also for sending godly men and women full of Your wisdom into my life for me to learn of Your ways.

Today's Thought

When I depend on God's wisdom, I will be blessed with fruitfulness and good success in all that I do.

Today's Reflection On Favor

_____

_____

_____

_____

The Wisdom Of Christ In Action

❖

Today's Scripture

But of him are ye in Christ Jesus, who of God is made unto us wisdom,
and righteousness, and sanctification, and redemption:
—1 Corinthians 1:30 KJV

BELOVED, WHEN YOU depend on God's wisdom to succeed today, you will see whatever you do prosper. Simply observe how our Lord Jesus always flowed in divine wisdom in His earthly ministry. For example, look at what happened when the Pharisees brought the woman caught in adultery to Him. The Pharisees came to Him and quoted from the law, saying, "Teacher, this woman was caught in adultery, in the very act. Now Moses, in the law, commanded us that such should be stoned. But what do You say?" (John 8:4–5).

Jesus, who is seated at the Father's right hand,
is "made unto us wisdom!"

They thought that they had succeeded in trapping Jesus because if He told them to stone her, then they would accuse Him of not demonstrating the forgiveness and grace that He had been preaching about. If He were to say that they should not stone her, then the Pharisees would accuse Him of breaking the law of Moses and bring a charge against Him.

The Pharisees were probably gloating over the clever trap that they had devised. That is why they confronted Jesus in the public area around the temple. They wanted to embarrass Him in front of the multitudes that had come to hear Him teach. Now, observe the wisdom of Jesus in operation. He simply told them, "He who is without sin among you, let him throw a stone at her first" (John 8:7).

What majesty! They came to Jesus with the law of Moses and Jesus gave them the perfect standard of the law. Without flinching, He simply challenged the person who was perfect before the law to cast the first stone. The Pharisees who had come to ensnare Jesus began to walk away one by one, completely silenced. This same Jesus, with all His wisdom, is today our ascended Christ, who is seated at the Father's right hand, and whom the Bible says is "made unto us wisdom!"

From this and other accounts of Jesus in the Gospels, we see how in everything He does, our Savior is altogether lovely. He is never early, never late. He is always at the right place at the right time. He is always in perfect peace and there is no sense of hurry about Him. When it was time to be tender, He was infinitely gentle, gracious and forgiving—we see this from His response to the woman caught in adultery (John 8:10–11). When it was time to overturn the tables of the money changers, He did it with passion. He was never frazzled by the Pharisees' attempts to trip Him up and was always flowing with divine wisdom. He is steel and velvet, meekness and majesty, perfect manhood and deity. This is Jesus and you are **in Him**! Begin to see yourself in Christ, who is always flowing with divine wisdom, always in control of the situation, and the same wisdom that flows in Him will flow in and through you.

❖

Today's Prayer

Father, thank You for placing me in Jesus, who is always flowing with divine wisdom. There is no problem that He cannot solve. Lord Jesus, as I go about my various activities today, I thank You that You are my wisdom. Thank You for leading and guiding me to say and do the right thing at the right time. I believe that things that are confusing or difficult to resolve in the natural will be resolved quickly because You are my wisdom!

Today's Thought
*I am in Christ who is always flowing
with divine wisdom!*

Today's Reflection On Favor

_____

_____

_____

_____

_____

_____

_____

_____

_____

_____

_____

_____

_____

_____

_____

_____

_____

_____

_____

_____

_____

Wisdom Is The Principal Thing

❖

Today's Scripture

*Wisdom is the principal thing; therefore get wisdom. And in
all your getting, get understanding. —Proverbs 4:7*

CHRIST IS MADE unto us **wisdom first**, then righteousness, holiness
and redemption (1 Corinthians 1:30). Wisdom comes first! Jesus as our
wisdom is given first importance. There is a difference between wisdom
and knowledge. Knowledge puffs up (1 Corinthians 8:1). It can make one
proud and arrogant. But wisdom will make you humble and teachable.
You can read extensively and accumulate a lot of knowledge, but still
lack wisdom. You also don't become wise just by growing older and
having more experience in life. Wisdom is not natural. It does not matter
if you are young or old, experienced or inexperienced, highly educated
or not. Wisdom comes by God's unmerited favor.

**Promotion and honor all come as a result of
receiving Jesus as your wisdom.**

Listen to what God's Word says about the importance of wisdom:
"Wisdom is the principal thing; therefore get wisdom. And in all your
getting, get understanding. Exalt her, and she will promote you; she will
bring you honor, when you embrace her. She will place on your head an
ornament of grace [unmerited favor]; a crown of glory she will deliver
to you" (Proverbs 4:7–9). You see, promotion and honor all come as a
result of receiving Jesus as your wisdom.

I remember how the key thing that I would pray for every day in
the early days of our church was for the wisdom of God to guide us in

everything that we did. That was my focus. I did not want to manage the church with my own human wisdom. I wanted to depend on Jesus' wisdom. In fact, it was during this time of believing for God's wisdom that the Lord opened my eyes to the gospel of grace!

When my eyes were opened to the gospel of Jesus' unmerited favor, lives began to be wonderfully changed and transformed, and from just a few hundred people in the mid-nineties, our highest attendance for our Sunday services to date was more than 22,000 precious people. Whenever I am asked to explain how we grew the church, my answer is plain and simple—it was and is entirely by the unmerited favor of Jesus. I know that it is grace and grace alone that caused our church to experience such explosive growth.

Before our church experienced such an explosion in numbers, the Lord asked me if I would do something. As I was spending time in His presence and reading His Word one day, He asked me if I would preach Jesus in every sermon. To be honest, my first thought then was that if I preached only Jesus in every message, many people would stop coming and the size of our church would shrink. Then, the Lord asked me, "If people stop coming, will you still preach Jesus in all your messages?" Like all young pastors, I was ambitious and wanted to grow the church, but I submitted to the Lord and said, "Yes, Lord, even if the church grows smaller, I will keep on preaching Jesus!"

Little did I know that this was actually a test from the Lord, because from the moment I began preaching Jesus, unveiling His loveliness and the perfection of His finished work every Sunday, as a church, we have never looked back. I didn't realize that throughout all those years of praying for wisdom, the wisdom of God would lead me to the unveiling of the gospel of grace—the gospel of grace that is unadulterated by the law and man's works, and based entirely on the finished work of Jesus. That is what wisdom does. It will always lead you to the person of Jesus and the cross!

Today, the same gospel of grace that we preach every Sunday in our church is being broadcast into millions of homes across America, Europe, the Middle East and the Asia Pacific region. We started as a little church in Singapore that nobody had heard of, but God's unmerited favor has blessed us to become an international ministry that is impacting the world with the good news of His unmerited favor. We take no credit for it because this wisdom is from Jesus, and our boast is in Him and Him alone. Beloved, let His wisdom lead you to supernatural success!

Today's Prayer

Father, I don't want to be puffed up with knowledge, but I want to walk and talk in Your wisdom. I thank You that Jesus, who lives in me by His Spirit, is already my wisdom. Today, I look to Him for wisdom and understanding. I thank You that His wisdom flows in me, giving me creative ideas, pointing out pitfalls to me and, most importantly, showing me more of His lovely person and finished work at the cross!

Today's Thought

Wisdom always leads me to the person of Jesus and His finished work at the cross.

Today's Reflection On Favor

_____

_____

_____

_____

_____

_____

_____

_____

The Spirit Of Wisdom

❖

Today's Scripture

That the God of our Lord Jesus Christ, the Father of glory, may give to you the spirit of wisdom and revelation in the knowledge of Him, the eyes of your understanding being enlightened; that you may know what is the hope of His calling, what are the riches of the glory of His inheritance in the saints, and what is the exceeding greatness of His power toward us who believe, according to the working of His mighty power.
—*Ephesians 1:17–19*

IF GOD TELLS us that wisdom is the principal thing, then it behooves us to know and operate in the "spirit of wisdom." But do you know what the "spirit of wisdom" is? Look at the prayer (above) that the apostle Paul prayed over the church in Ephesus. The spirit of wisdom and revelation is in **the knowledge of Jesus**! The more you know Jesus and have a revelation of His unmerited favor in your life, the more you will have the spirit of wisdom. I challenge you to pray this prayer for wisdom on a regular basis because when you increase in the knowledge of Jesus, He will surely lead you to good success in every aspect of your life.

The more you know Jesus and have a revelation of His unmerited favor in your life, the more you will have the spirit of wisdom.

Note that when Paul was praying this prayer for the believers in Ephesus, they were already filled with the Holy Spirit. But Paul still prayed that God would give them a spirit of wisdom and revelation in their knowledge of Jesus. It is one thing to have the Holy Spirit inside you, but it is another thing to let the Holy Spirit inside you flow as the spirit of wisdom and revelation. And as you pray to be led by the spirit of wisdom today, be confident that you will experience the Holy Spirit leading you in Jesus' divine and unmatched wisdom. When the Holy Spirit leads you in the wisdom of Jesus, there will be no impossible situation, no insolvable problem and no insurmountable crisis. The wisdom of Jesus in you will help you to successfully navigate all your trials and cause you to prevail over all your challenges!

❖

Today's Prayer

Father, please give me the spirit of wisdom and revelation to know Jesus better. Open the eyes of my understanding and enlighten me, so that I may know the hope to which He has called me, the riches of His glorious inheritance in the saints and the exceeding greatness of His power toward those who believe. Father, lead me in the wisdom of Christ in all that I do today.

Today's Thought

The wisdom of Jesus in me helps me to prevail over all my trials and challenges.

Today's Reflection On Favor

_____

_____

_____

_____

_____

_____

_____

_____

_____

DAY 82

The Secret To Solomon's Wisdom

❖

Today's Scripture

Therefore give to Your servant an understanding heart to judge Your people, that I may discern between good and evil. For who is able to judge this great people of Yours? —1 Kings 3:9

LET'S TAKE A look at the life of Solomon. When Solomon became king, he was only a young man of about 18 years old and had big shoes to fill as David's successor to the throne. Solomon was not filled with wisdom when he first ascended the throne, but he was clearly very earnest. He went to Mount Gibeon, where the tabernacle of Moses was, to offer a thousand burnt offerings to the Lord. At Mount Gibeon, the Lord appeared to Solomon in a dream and said, "Ask! What shall I give you?" (2 Chronicles 1:7).

With the wisdom of Jesus, you won't only be blessed, but you will also be able to hold on to the blessings in your life.

Now, think about this for a moment. What would you have asked for if you were in Solomon's position? Solomon did not ask for riches. Neither did he ask to be honored by all men. Instead, he told the Lord, "...give me **wisdom and knowledge**, that I may go out and come in before this people; for who can judge this great people of Yours?" (2 Chronicles 1:10).

The Bible records that Solomon's request "pleased the Lord" (1 Kings 3:10) and the Lord replied, "Because this was in your heart, and you have not asked riches or wealth or honor or the life of your enemies, nor have you asked long life—but have asked wisdom and knowledge for yourself, that you may judge My people over whom I have made you king—wisdom and knowledge are granted to you; and I will give you riches and wealth and honor, such as none of the kings have had who were before you, nor shall any after you have the like" (2 Chronicles 1:11–12).

The Book of 1 Kings tells us that Solomon told the Lord, "Therefore give to Your servant an **understanding heart** to judge Your people, that I may discern between good and evil. For who is able to judge this great people of Yours?" So when Solomon asked for wisdom and knowledge, he was asking for an understanding heart.

Let's go deeper. The word "understanding" here is the Hebrew word *shama*, which means "to hear intelligently."[1] In other words, Solomon had asked for a **hearing heart**—one that hears from and flows with the leading of the Spirit of God, who leads us into all truth (John 16:13). You need a hearing heart for God's wisdom to flow through you in every aspect of your life!

I believe that the same request that pleased the Lord then still pleases Him today. God is pleased when we ask Jesus for wisdom. To ask Him for wisdom is to put ourselves in a posture of trusting and depending on His unmerited favor. Only the humble can ask Jesus for wisdom and a hearing heart.

Although Solomon only asked for wisdom, the Lord added "riches and wealth and honor" to him. Too many people are chasing riches, wealth and honor, not realizing that they come through the wisdom of Jesus. Even if someone were to come into sudden wealth, without the wisdom of Jesus to manage it, the money would be squandered away. But with the wisdom of Jesus, you won't only be blessed, you will also be able to hold on to the blessings in your life. Jesus makes you safe for good success that produces lasting and abiding fruit from generation to generation!

❖

Today's Prayer

Father, I ask for the same thing that King Solomon asked—an understanding or hearing heart. I want to be able to hear Your words of life and understand Your directions for my life, so that I can walk in Your wisdom. I want to be able to flow with Your Spirit, who guides me into all truth. Lead me to walk in Your wisdom in all things, so that I can live victoriously the life that You have given me and fulfill the calling that You have for me.

Today's Thought

Having a hearing heart allows me to know and walk in God's wisdom.

Today's Reflection On Favor

_____

_____

_____

_____

_____

_____

_____

_____

_____

_____

_____

_____

_____

_____

Wisdom And Length Of Days

❖

Today's Scripture

Happy is the man who finds wisdom, and the man who gains
understanding…Length of days is in her right hand, in her
left hand riches and honor. —Proverbs 3:13, 16

THE BIBLE PROMISES something when you have wisdom: "Happy is the
man who finds wisdom...**Length of days is in her right hand**, in her
left hand riches and honor." Unfortunately, for King Solomon, he only
had the left hand of wisdom, which holds riches and honor. The Lord
had said to him, "…**if** you walk in My ways, to keep My statutes and My
commandments…then **I will lengthen your days**" (1 Kings 3:14).

Because of Jesus' finished work on the cross, riches and
honor, as well as length of days, belong to us!

For Solomon, who was under the old covenant of law, the blessing
of length of days was a conditional one, which he could receive only
if he was able to keep the law perfectly. However, Solomon failed to
do so and he did not enjoy length of days, which is in wisdom's right
hand.

Today, because we are under the new covenant of grace, Jesus is at
the Father's right hand and He is our wisdom. And when we have Jesus,
we can be blessed with the two hands of wisdom because of His finished
work on the cross. This means that riches and honor, as well as length of
days, belong to us! What an awesome God we serve!

Beloved, pursue Jesus and you will experience wisdom in every area
of your life. You cannot try to earn, deserve or study to acquire God's
wisdom. It comes by His unmerited favor. His wisdom will give you

good success in your career. It will cause you to succeed as a student, parent or spouse.

For instance, if you are facing some problems in your marriage, God will not just "zap" your spouse and make him or her do a moonwalk and come back to you! The same thing that drove your spouse away from you in the first place will just drive him or her away again. What you need is wisdom for your marital situation!

If you are faced with a crisis in your business, depend on the Lord for His wisdom. There are no "money problems," only "idea problems." Trust that the Lord will bless you with the wisdom from heaven to cause everything that you touch at your workplace to prosper. God's wisdom always leads to promotion and good success.

Today's Prayer

Father, I thank You that because of Jesus' finished work at the cross, I am blessed with both the left and right hand of wisdom—riches and honor as well as length of days belong to me! I know that You want to bless me and my family with good success, and I thank You for making Your wisdom that brings this good success available to me through Your unmerited favor.

Today's Thought

When I trust the Lord to bless me with wisdom, promotion and good success will follow.

Today's Reflection On Favor

_____

_____

_____

_____

_____

God's Wisdom
Brings You Promotion

❖

Today's Scripture

Then Pharaoh said to Joseph, "Inasmuch as God has shown you all this, there is no one as discerning and wise as you. You shall be over my house, and all my people shall be ruled according to your word; only in regard to the throne will I be greater than you." —Genesis 41:39–40

IN GENESIS 39:3–4, we see how when Potiphar saw that the Lord was with Joseph, and that everything he touched prospered, Potiphar immediately promoted Joseph and placed him in charge over all the affairs of his house. Similarly, when Pharaoh saw that the Spirit of God was in Joseph and that there was none who was as wise and as discerning as Joseph, Pharaoh placed him in charge of the whole of Egypt (Genesis 41:38–41).

If you are caught in a situation where you don't know what to do, it is time to humble yourself and ask the Lord for wisdom.

My friend, I want you to note this: Joseph **knew** that God was the source of his wisdom. When Pharaoh said, "I have had a dream, and there is no one who can interpret it. But I have heard it said of you that you can understand a dream, to interpret it," Joseph immediately replied, "It is not in me; God will give Pharaoh an answer of peace" (Genesis 41:15–16). Joseph knew that his wisdom was a result of the Lord's unmerited favor and would not take any credit for it. Clearly, here was a man who understood grace, and could be trusted with increase, promotion and more good success.

Observe the wisdom of Joseph in action. Joseph did not just interpret Pharaoh's dream. He went on to advise Pharaoh on how to take advantage of the seven years of abundance to prepare for the seven years of famine that were revealed in his dream. Did you notice how Joseph's wise advice led to the creation of a position of influence for himself? That is how the wisdom of the Lord operates. Proverbs 18:16 says, "A man's gift makes room for him, and brings him before great men." Joseph knew that his wisdom was a gift from the Lord. He knew that he did not earn it and that it flowed from the Lord's unmerited favor toward him.

The Lord's ways are amazing. See the extent of Joseph's promotion in Genesis 41. In the space of less than an hour, he rose from a lowly prisoner to the highest possible office in all of Egypt. That, my friend, is the unmerited favor of God! No striving, no self-effort, no compromises and no manipulation, just pure grace and grace alone made all the difference in Joseph's life!

Remember that when the Lord is with you, you are a successful person. It may feel like you are in a prison now, stuck in a hopeless situation, cast away and forgotten like Joseph was, but the story is not over yet! The Lord's promotion is around the corner. Whatever situation you are in right now, do not give up.

If you are caught in a situation where you don't know what to do, it is time to humble yourself and ask the Lord for wisdom. The Bible says, "If any of you lacks wisdom, let him ask of God, who gives to all liberally and without reproach, and it will be given to him" (James 1:5). To ask the Lord for wisdom is to say, "I can't, Lord, but You can. I give up on my own efforts and depend entirely upon your unmerited favor and wisdom." As you receive His wisdom, riches and honor, as well as long life, will follow after you. Run to Him right now!

❖

Today's Prayer

Father, I acknowledge that any godly wisdom that I have today is a result of Your unmerited favor. I thank You that if I need more wisdom, all I have to do is ask You for it, and You will gladly give it to me. And because You are willing to give me more wisdom, I don't have to strive, struggle and stress myself out to get ahead in life. Just a drop of Your wisdom and favor can cause me to be quickly promoted to a position of influence and power!

Today's Thought

If I need wisdom, I can just ask God for it—
He gives it liberally and without reproach!

Today's Reflection On Favor

_____

_____

_____

_____

_____

_____

_____

_____

_____

_____

_____

_____

_____

_____

DAY 85

Wisdom Makes You Value Jesus' Presence

❖

Today's Scripture

Then Solomon awoke; and indeed it had been a dream. And he came to Jerusalem and stood before the ark of the covenant of the Lord, offered up burnt offerings, offered peace offerings, and made a feast for all his servants. —1 Kings 3:15

LET'S SEE WHAT King Solomon did right after he received wisdom from God in a dream. David had instituted worship at Mount Zion, not at Mount Gibeon. What were left in the tabernacle of Moses at Mount Gibeon were merely the physical objects, structure and form. It had the lampstand, table of showbread and altar of incense. But the most important furniture in the tabernacle, the ark of the covenant, which had the presence of God, was missing.

When you receive God's wisdom, you will want to receive even more from God's Word and from the presence of Jesus.

King David had a special revelation of the ark of the covenant and had brought it back to Jerusalem and placed it on Mount Zion. We see that for some reason, Solomon was into tradition before he received wisdom. While he was sincere in seeking the Lord at Mount Gibeon, the Lord's presence was actually at Mount Zion. The tabernacle of Moses only had the form, but the substance of the presence of the Lord was with the ark of the covenant in Jerusalem. But notice this: Once Solomon had received wisdom from the Lord, the **first thing** that he did when he awoke was to go to Jerusalem where he "stood before the ark of the covenant of the Lord, offered up burnt offerings, offered peace offerings, and made a feast for all his servants."

How can you tell if somebody has received wisdom from the Lord? The first thing that he will do is value the presence of Jesus! Once Solomon was inundated with God's wisdom, he left the formal structure in the tabernacle of Moses and went to look for the Lord's presence in Jerusalem. After receiving wisdom and a hearing heart, he valued and treasured the Lord's presence. In the same way, when you receive God's wisdom, it will not draw you away from church. Instead, it will cause you to want to receive even more from God's Word and from the presence of Jesus.

"Pastor Prince, what is so significant about the ark of the covenant?"

The ark of the covenant is a picture of Jesus. It is made of wood, which speaks of Jesus' humanity (Isaiah 55:12; Mark 8:24), and it is overlaid with gold, which speaks of Jesus' divinity (Isaiah 2:20; Song of Solomon 5:11, 14–15). Jesus is 100 percent Man and 100 percent God. In the ark are three items: The stone tablets of the Ten Commandments, Aaron's rod, which had budded, and a golden pot of manna. These items represent man's failure and rebellion against God's perfect law, His appointed leadership and His provision, respectively.[1]

Now, look at God's heart for His people. He gave instructions that these symbols of man's rebellion be placed inside the ark and covered with the mercy seat! The mercy seat is where the high priest would sprinkle the blood of the offering to cover all the failings and rebellion of the children of Israel.

The ark of the covenant is but a shadow. Today, we have the substance of the finished work of Jesus at the cross, where the blood of God's own Son, not the inferior blood of bulls and goats, was shed to blot out **all** our sins, failings and rebellion **once and for all**!

It is no wonder that in battles in which the children of Israel **appreciated the value** of the ark, they emerged victorious. In the same way today, it is a clear indication of God's wisdom upon your life when you value and appreciate the person of Jesus and what He did for you at the cross. And because the true ark of the covenant is with you all the time, you can't help but be triumphant, successful and victorious in any battle that you may be in. Solomon realized this and immediately pursued the presence of the Lord after he awoke from his dream. My friend, go after the presence of Jesus in your life. He is your wisdom and victory over every battle today!

Today's Prayer

Father, Your Word declares that Jesus will never leave me nor forsake me. Therefore, right now, Jesus, I acknowledge and thank You for Your abiding presence. And just as the Israelites were always victorious in battles when Your presence was with them, I expect to see victory today in any challenge that I face because You are with me. Thank You, Jesus, for giving me wisdom, victory, lasting success and peace.

Today's Thought

When I go after and appreciate the presence of Jesus, I can't help but be triumphant, successful and victorious in any battle.

Today's Reflection On Favor

_____

_____

_____

_____

_____

_____

_____

_____

_____

Make Jesus Your Priority And See Blessings Added To You

❖

Today's Scripture

Therefore do not worry, saying, "What shall we eat?" or "What shall we drink?" or "What shall we wear?"...For your heavenly Father knows that you need all these things. But seek first the kingdom of God and His righteousness, and all these things shall be added to you.
—*Matthew 6:31–33*

WHEN I TALK about not worrying and keeping our eyes on Jesus, some people think that I am not being practical. Beloved, you can worry all you like about your current crisis, but it will not improve or change your situation one bit. Please understand that I am not making light of what you are going through. I am just offering you the best solution I know that works. Your breakthrough will not come as a result of your struggling. It will come when you rest in the person of Jesus and His finished work.

The Lord loads us with benefits daily!

Jesus said, "...do not worry about your life, what you will eat or what you will drink; nor about your body, what you will put on..." (Matthew 6:25). Now, Jesus was not saying that these things—food, drink and clothing—are not important. In fact, He says that "your heavenly Father knows that you need all these things." But what Jesus wants us to do is to "seek first the kingdom of God and His righteousness," and He promises that "all these things shall be added to you."

Now, who is God's righteousness? Jesus Christ. And who is the king of the "kingdom of God" that we are to seek? Jesus Christ (Revelation 19:16)! Jesus was actually referring to Himself when He was preaching this. When you seek Him first in your life and make Him your priority each day, all these material provisions—what you will eat, drink and wear—will be added to you. God does not delight in taking things away from you. He delights in adding to you, increasing you, promoting you and enriching you. Psalm 68:19 says, "Blessed be the Lord, who **daily** loads us with benefits..." The Lord loads us with benefits daily! That is how good our Savior is. His mercies and His unmerited favor are new every morning. That is the way to live and enjoy life, knowing that Jesus is *with you* and *for you* every step of the way.

Put Jesus first in everything that you do. Honor Him and give Him preeminence in your daily life. Partake of His finished work daily by reading His living words to you. Practice the presence of Jesus and be conscious that He is with you, the same way that Joseph in the Bible was conscious that the Lord was with Him. Jesus will bless the works of your hands, and everything you touch will indeed prosper and bring good success into your life.

❖

Today's Prayer

Father, I thank You that You are well aware of all the things I need in this life, and You want to ADD these things to me, and not keep them from me. Help me, therefore, not to worry about or focus on getting these things, but help me make seeking Jesus and His righteousness my first priority every day. Lord Jesus, I want to put You first in everything that I do. I know that when I give You first place in my life, everything else will fall into place for my good!

Today's Thought

When I put Jesus first in everything I do,
whatever I touch will prosper!

Today's Reflection On Favor

_____

_____

_____

_____

_____

_____

_____

_____

_____

_____

_____

_____

_____

_____

_____

_____

_____

_____

_____

_____

DAY 87

Do The One Thing That Is Needful

❖

Today's Scripture

And Jesus answered and said to her, "Martha, Martha, you are worried and troubled about many things. But one thing is needed, and Mary has chosen that good part, which will not be taken away from her."
—Luke 10:41–42

Is it practical to be occupied with Jesus? Does it help you? Does it put food on the table? Does it prosper your finances? Does it make your physical body healthy? We know what it did for Peter—he walked on water. Now, let's take a look at what it did for Mary. You can find the story of Mary and her sister, Martha, in Luke 10:38–42.

The one thing that is needful is for you to sit at Jesus' feet and keep your eyes, ears and heart on Him.

Mary was seated at Jesus' feet when the Lord came to visit them. Martha, the elder sister, was busy working in the kitchen, making sure that everything was in order and ensuring that there was enough food and drink for their guest. Who was Martha busy serving? Jesus. And while Martha was frantically running in and out of the kitchen, what was her younger sister Mary doing? In the midst of all the busyness and activity, Mary was sitting at Jesus' feet, beholding His beauty, beholding His glory and hanging on to every word that proceeded from His lips. While Mary was resting and drawing living water from Jesus, her sister Martha was restless, frantic and stressed from serving Jesus. One sister was focused on serving, while the other was focused on receiving.

Look what happened after a while. Martha's stress from serving finally led to this outburst of frustration: "Lord, do You not care that my sister has left me to serve alone? Therefore tell her to help me" (Luke 10:40). In one moment of anger, she blamed two persons: The Lord Jesus as well as her sister Mary. Now, listen closely to Jesus' response, and you may just find yourself in the Lord's description of Martha: "Martha, Martha, you are worried and troubled about many things. But one thing is needed, and Mary has chosen that good part, which will not be taken away from her."

This is an amazing response. In Middle Eastern culture, it was right for Mary to be in the kitchen preparing food and serving her guest. Now, it would have been a shameful thing for Mary to sit at Jesus' feet and not help Martha if Jesus was just an ordinary guest. But Jesus was no ordinary guest and Mary knew it. He was God in the flesh and the greatest way you can minister to God when He is in your home is to sit at His feet and keep drawing from Him! That is what delights our Lord.

When you come to Jesus to draw as much as you can from Him, He loves it. That is why Jesus was pleased with Mary. That is why He defended Mary's action, saying, "...one thing is needed, and Mary has chosen that good part..." What is the "one thing" that is needful? Is it to busy yourself in serving the Lord? Is it to be troubled about many things? No, the one thing that is needful is for you to sit at Jesus' feet and keep your eyes, ears and heart on Him. One sister saw Jesus in the natural, needing her ministry. The other sister saw Him as God veiled in flesh with a fullness to draw upon. Which sister do you suppose complimented Jesus and made Him feel like the God that He is? Mary. Martha obviously forgot that this God-Man multiplied loaves and fishes to feed a multitude. **He has not come to be fed but to feed!**

Unfortunately, sometimes, the hardest thing for us to do is to sit down! Sometimes, the most challenging thing we can do is to cease from our own efforts and rest solely on Jesus' unmerited favor. Often, we are like Martha—worried, busy and troubled about many things. It can all be legitimate things that we are worried about. In Martha's case, she was trying her best to serve the Lord. She ended up doing many things that day, but missed out on doing the **one** thing that was actually needful.

Believers who do that one thing that is needful are not worried about anything else. On the other hand, believers who fail to do that **one** thing end up being troubled about **many** things. Do you believe that only one thing is needful—to rest at Jesus' feet and receive from Him?

Now, is it practical to just be occupied with Jesus? Absolutely. We find that later, in the Gospel of John, Mary took a pound of very costly oil of spikenard, anointed the feet of Jesus and wiped His feet with her hair to prepare Him for His burial (John 12:3–8). On resurrection morning, some women came with ointment to anoint Jesus' body, but it was too late then. They were doing the right thing, but at the wrong time. The Lord had already risen. But Mary did the right thing at the right time. This shows us that when you do the one thing that is needful, you will end up doing the right thing at the right time, and God will cause all that you touch to be amazingly blessed.

Like Mary, choose to focus on the beauty, glory and love of Jesus. Choose not to be troubled about many things or constantly occupied with yourself. Like Peter, turn away from the storm and look at Jesus, and you will start walking above the storm. Beloved, choose to focus on the Lord and rest in His finished work. As Jesus is, so are you in this world!

❖

Today's Prayer

Lord Jesus, although I have many things to do today, I choose to sit at Your feet and to receive from You. Minister Your words of life to me! I want to draw from You and drink of You. I thank You that when I spend time at Your feet, You will put me at the right place at the right time and cause me to prosper and enjoy good success!

Today's Thought

When I do the one thing that is needful, I will end up doing the right thing at the right time.

Today's Reflection On Favor

_____

_____

_____

_____

_____

_____

_____

_____

_____

_____

_____

_____

_____

_____

_____

_____

_____

_____

_____

_____

Be Righteousness-Conscious And Experience Every Blessing

Today's Scripture

"No weapon formed against you shall prosper, and every tongue which rises against you in judgment you shall condemn. This is the heritage of the servants of the Lord, and their righteousness is from Me," says the Lord.
—Isaiah 54:17

Have you noticed how it is usually only the first part of Isaiah 54:17 that is quoted: "No weapon formed against you shall prosper"? Now, do you want to know the secret to unleashing this promise of protection and walking fully in your inheritance in Christ? Interestingly, this verse is rarely quoted in full: "'No weapon formed against you shall prosper, and every tongue which rises against you in judgment you shall condemn. This is the heritage of the servants of the Lord, and **their righteousness is from Me**,' says the Lord." You see, beloved, it is when you know that your righteousness is from the Lord that no weapon formed against you will prosper, and every tongue of accusation, judgment and condemnation that rises against you will fail!

God wants you to use your faith to believe that even when you have failed, He is a God who justifies the ungodly and makes them righteous. This is grace.

For many of us, it is easy to confess that you are righteous when everything is going well. But let's talk about the times when you are faced with a crisis at home or at work, when you have made a mistake, when you are sick, when you are tempted or when you are depressed. That is when the devil, who is the "accuser of our brethren" (Revelation 12:10), will come against you and scream accusatory thoughts of condemnation in your ears: "You call yourself a Christian? You think that God will hear your prayer this time?"

My friend, **that** is the time to start speaking your righteousness, and no weapon formed against you shall prosper. Instead, you will walk in all your inheritance in Christ, which includes the blessings of Abraham. The accuser wants you to focus on your performance, and if you go into the realm of the law, faith is made void and the promise made of no effect (Romans 4:14). But if you maintain your belief and confession that you are righteous in Christ, the promise to Abraham and all the blessings of being an heir of the world will be unleashed into every aspect of your life.

The accuser is very subtle. He has no problems with you using your faith for other things, like a new car or promotion, as long as you don't use your faith for the most important thing—believing that you are righteous by faith in Jesus. Once you focus and channel all your faith in that direction, not only will the accuser lose his power over you, all the blessings that you desire will also be added to you! As God's Word promises, "...seek **first** the kingdom of God and His righteousness, and all these things shall be **added** to you" (Matthew 6:33).

"But Pastor Prince, I...I don't deserve Abraham's blessing."

You are absolutely right, my friend. None of us deserve the blessing of Abraham and that is why it is important that we know that we are righteous by faith. We are not getting what our own righteousness deserves. We are getting what Jesus' righteousness deserves. We did nothing right, but Jesus did everything right on our behalf. This is grace—God's undeserved, unearned and unmerited favor. His grace is the key to becoming an heir of the world and to experience the full blessings of Abraham.

You need to read this portion of the Scriptures for yourself:

For if Abraham was justified by works, he has something to boast about, but not before God. For what does the Scripture say? "Abraham believed God, and it was accounted to him for righteousness." Now to him who works, the wages are not counted as grace but as debt. **But to him who does not work but believes on Him who justifies the ungodly, his faith is accounted for righteousness**.

—Romans 4:2–5

The secret to Abraham's blessings is found in verse five (see bolded part). What did Abraham believe? He believed that God justifies the ungodly. Take some time to meditate on this. God wants you to use your faith to believe that even when you have failed, He is a God who justifies the ungodly and makes them righteous. This is grace.

My friend, put your faith in His unmerited favor instead of your works. Being righteous is not based on your perfect performance. It is based on His perfect work. Your part is to use your faith to believe that you are indeed righteous by faith, so that you will reign in this life, become an heir of the world, and live an overcoming and victorious life.

❖

Today's Prayer

Father, I declare that even when I have failed, no weapon formed against me will prosper because I have the righteousness of Jesus Christ. Every tongue that rises up against me in judgment and condemnation, I have the right to condemn because I am righteous in Christ. And because I have Your gift of righteousness, I will reign in life through Christ. I will enjoy Abraham's blessing and live an overcoming and victorious life!

Today's Thought

*No weapon formed against me can prosper because
I am the righteousness of God in Christ!*

Today's Reflection On Favor

_____

_____

_____

_____

_____

_____

_____

_____

_____

_____

_____

_____

_____

_____

_____

_____

_____

_____

_____

_____

_____

_____

DAY 89

The Righteousness Of Faith Speaks

❖

Today's Scripture

*For Moses writes about the righteousness which is of the law,
"The man who does those things shall live by them." But the
righteousness of faith speaks... —Romans 10:5–6*

LET ME SAY something about faith. You cannot have faith without speaking it. When you study Romans 10, you will notice that it says that "the righteousness which is of the law...**does**...But the righteousness of faith **speaks**." The law is about doing, whereas faith is about speaking. It is not enough to just know in your mind that you are righteous. It is not enough to just read this chapter or hear a sermon on righteousness and mentally agree that you are righteous. You need to open your mouth and say by faith, "I am the righteousness of God in Christ." This is where many believers are missing out on the blessing of Abraham. They are not speaking their righteousness by faith.

**Our first response when we discover a symptom in
our body, when we receive a bad report or when
we are faced with a trial, should always be to say,
"I am the righteousness of God in Christ."**

Our first response to a trying situation is very important. Our first response when we discover a symptom in our body, when we receive a bad report or when we are faced with a trial, should always be to say, "I am the righteousness of God in Christ." Come on now, this is where the rubber meets the road. This is when we need to speak it. You need to not only know that you are righteous, you need to believe and speak your righteousness in Christ. It is not faith until you speak it! Paul said, "And since we have the same spirit of faith, according to what is written, 'I believed and therefore I spoke,' we also believe and therefore speak" (2 Corinthians 4:13). The spirit of faith is clearly about believing and speaking. So it does not matter how many sermons or books on righteousness you have heard and read. You need to believe it and speak it.

When you fail and fall short of the law's perfect standard, that is the time you should exercise your faith to say, "I am the righteousness of God in Christ." At that very moment when you are seething in anger at your spouse, or when you have just lost your cool on the road, it takes faith to say that you are righteous because you know that you have missed it. And you know what? The moment you say it, even if you are still in the midst of your anger, you will feel like you have ushered something good into that situation. You take a step back and start to relax, and the anger dissipates as you begin to realize your true identity in Christ.

Men, if you see a scantily clad woman on television or on the cover of a magazine and you are tempted, what is your first response? Are you sin-conscious or righteousness-conscious? Sin-consciousness will draw you to succumb to your temptation, whereas righteousness-consciousness gives you the power to overcome every temptation. That is why the enemy wants to keep you sin-conscious. Confessing your sins all the time keeps you sin-conscious. It is as if Jesus did not become your sin on the cross. Righteousness-consciousness keeps you conscious of Jesus. Every time you speak it, you magnify the work of Jesus on the cross. So believe and speak the truth: "I am the righteousness of God in Christ." Then, you cannot help but see the results of magnifying the Lord Jesus and His finished work!

Today's Prayer

Father, because of Jesus' perfect sacrifice for me at the cross, I am always righteous in Your sight. Help me to always be mindful of my everlasting righteousness in Christ and to confess it in every situation I face. Because I am righteous in Christ, I am empowered by Your Spirit to overcome every challenge and reign in life!

Today's Thought

Righteousness-consciousness gives me the power to overcome all odds.

Today's Reflection On Favor

_____

_____

_____

_____

_____

_____

_____

_____

_____

_____

_____

_____

_____

How To Increase In God's Unmerited Favor

❖

Today's Scripture

Therefore, having been justified by faith, we have peace with God through our Lord Jesus Christ, through whom also we have access by faith into this grace in which we stand, and rejoice in hope of the glory of God.
—*Romans 5:1–2*

GOD'S WORD TELLS us that "Jesus **increased** in **wisdom** and stature, and in **favor** with God and men" (Luke 2:52). This is a good verse to pray and speak over your children—that they first increase in favor with God, and then in favor with man. Your "vertical relationship" with God should always be given priority over your "horizontal relationship" with the people around you.

Because of Jesus' perfect work on the cross, you are righteous by His blood, and you are greatly blessed, highly favored and deeply loved!

Like Jesus, you can increase in wisdom and in God's unmerited favor. How? You have probably noticed that some believers seem to experience a lot more unmerited favor than others. I believe that this is because these believers understand the key to accessing God's favor. Romans 5:2 clearly spells out that "we have access by faith into this grace [unmerited favor] in which we stand." To gain access to your computer or your bank account, you need a password. To gain access to and increase in God's unmerited favor, the "password" or key that we need to have is faith, faith to believe that YOU, _____ (insert your name), **are** highly favored!

One of the things that I have taught my church members to do is to declare over themselves that they are **greatly blessed, highly favored and deeply loved**.

"How do we know that we are greatly blessed, Pastor Prince?"

Read Hebrews 6:13–14 for yourself. God wanted us to be so anchored in the sure and steadfast knowledge that He **will** bless us, the seed of Abraham, that He swore by Himself, saying, "Surely blessing I will bless you, and multiplying I will multiply you."

"How can we say that we are highly favored?"

Ephesians 1:6 tells us that by God's grace (unmerited favor), God "made us **accepted** in the Beloved." In the original Greek text, the word "accepted" is the word *charitoo*, which means "highly favored."[1]

"And are we really deeply loved by God?"

God didn't just love us. John 3:16 says that "God **so** loved the world that He gave His only begotten Son." He demonstrated how He SO loved us when He sent Jesus to die on the cross for us.

I pray that the verses that I have shown you here will help you believe that through Jesus, you are indeed greatly blessed, highly favored and deeply loved. If these truths are still not established in your heart, start speaking them. Look at yourself in the mirror every morning and declare boldly, "Because of Jesus' perfect work on the cross, I am righteous by His blood, and I am greatly blessed, highly favored and deeply loved! I expect good things to come my way. I expect good success and I have a confident expectation of good!"

Once you receive Christ, **you** are standing on favor ground. You are no longer on condemnation ground. God looks on you as His favorite child!

"But Pastor Prince, how can God have so many favorites?"

Hey, He is God. Don't try to limit an infinite God with your finite mind. The Bible tells us that God counts the very hairs on each of our heads (Matthew 10:30). (I love my daughter very much, but I have never counted the number of strands of hair on her head.) His love for each of us is intimate and deeply personal. In His eyes, we are all His favorites!

❖

Today's Prayer

Father, establish me in the truth that I am greatly blessed, highly favored and deeply loved. Because of Your unmerited favor and Jesus' perfect work on the cross, I am righteous by His blood. I believe and declare that I am greatly blessed, highly favored and deeply loved! Today, I expect good things to come my way. I expect good success! Hallelujah! Thank You, Father, for Your unmerited favor!

Today's Thought

I am God's favorite!

Today's Reflection On Favor

_____

_____

_____

_____

_____

_____

_____

_____

_____

_____

_____

_____

God Chooses The Weak To Bring Down The Mighty

❖

Today's Scripture

For you see your calling, brethren, that not many wise according to the flesh, not many mighty, not many noble, are called. But God has chosen the foolish things of the world to put to shame the wise, and God has chosen the weak things of the world to put to shame the things which are mighty. —1 Corinthians 1:26–27

GOD IS INTERESTED in your success. Even if you are not the swiftest, strongest, wisest, most knowledgeable and most skillful in the natural, God can still bless you with good success when you depend on His grace. You can rise above the system of meritocracy through His undeserved, unearned and unmerited favor. The system of the world only rewards the strong, while those who are weak are neglected and in some cases, even despised. But, in Jesus, there is hope for the weak.

In God's hands of grace, the foolish and weak things become even wiser and mightier than the wise and mighty things of the world.

God's way is completely opposite from the world's way. According to 1 Corinthians 1:26, "not many wise according to the flesh, not many mighty, not many noble, are called." Isn't it fascinating to discover that while the world looks favorably upon the wise, mighty and noble, God does not? Let's see in the next verse what God chooses instead: "God has chosen the **foolish things** of the world to put to shame the wise, and God has chosen the **weak things** of the world to put to shame the things which are mighty."

Isn't it amazing? God has chosen the foolish and weak things to qualify for His abundant blessings. But the verse does not say that the foolish and weak things will remain foolish and weak. Instead, by God's unmerited favor, they will put to shame the so-called wise and mighty things in this world. In His hands of grace, the foolish and weak things become even wiser and mightier than the wise and mighty things of the world.

This is something I have experienced personally. In high school, I was a stutterer. I watched the other kids talking and reading aloud in class effortlessly while I had serious trouble getting words out of my mouth.

I remember how there was this teacher who would come into class, and always get me to stand and read aloud in class. He did this just for the sheer pleasure of watching me stammer and stutter, knowing full well what would happen. And true enough, while I tried to get the first word out—"th- th- th- th- the," my classmates (especially the girls) would laugh, this teacher would laugh, and my ears would burn and turn red. This would happen every time he asked me to read in class.

Honestly, if you had told me then that I would be preaching to thousands of people every week, I would have run for cover under the table and said, "Get thee behind me, Satan!" If there was an area anyone who knew me back then believed I would fail in, it would have to be public speaking. But God looked down and said, "I am going to make a preacher out of this boy."

One day, when I was tired of being miserable, I told the Lord, "Lord, I don't have much to give You, but whatever I have I give You." I remember how my voice was the thing that embarrassed me the most, so I said, "Lord, I give You my voice." When I said that, I pitied Him for getting someone like me who had so many weaknesses.

To cut a long story short, after I gave all my weaknesses to the Lord, something supernatural happened. I stopped being conscious of my stuttering and it supernaturally disappeared. In the area of my weakness,

God supplied His strength. About two years ago, one of the teachers from my high school days came to my church and sat in one of the services I was preaching in. After the service, she wrote me a note that said, "I see a miracle. This must be God!"

Why does the Lord choose foolish and weak things to confound the wise and mighty things of this world? The answer is simple. It's so that **"no flesh should glory in His presence"** (1 Corinthians 1:29). God chooses the things that are weak in the natural so that no man can boast of his **own** ability—all glory redounds to the Lord.

I believe that the reason God chose someone like me to preach the gospel is so that others (especially those who had known me before) would look at me and say, "This must be God!" and God gets the glory. Now, seeing how God has used my voice, my main weakness, to bring life transformation and miracles not only to people in Singapore, but also around the world through our television broadcasts, I feel humbled because I know what I was like before God touched me. My friend, it is those who are proud and who depend on their human strength that God cannot use. So when you look at yourself and see only weaknesses, depend on God's unmerited favor and know that God can and will use you!

❖

Today's Prayer

Father, You know all about my weaknesses. Yet, You are willing to use me for Your purposes and glory. Therefore, I give You all my weaknesses and lean wholly on Your unmerited favor. In Your hands, those weaknesses will become strengths. Thank You for Your unmerited favor that will cause me to rise above the world's system of meritocracy and experience success beyond my natural abilities, experience and qualifications!

Even if I am not the smartest or strongest, God can bless me with good success when I depend on His unmerited favor.

Today's Reflection On Favor

_____

_____

_____

_____

_____

_____

_____

_____

_____

_____

_____

_____

_____

_____

_____

_____

_____

_____

_____

_____

_____

_____

DAY 92

When God Can Use You

❖

Today's Scripture

But of Him you are in Christ Jesus, who became for us wisdom from
God—and righteousness and sanctification and redemption—that,
as it is written, "He who glories, let him glory in the Lord."
—*1 Corinthians 1:30–31*

It is Jesus, His wisdom in your life, His righteousness and His perfect redemptive work on the cross that make you a success. So when you boast of your success, you can boast only in Jesus. Without Jesus, you have nothing to boast about. But with Jesus in your life, you can boast in Him and Him alone for every success and blessing that comes through His unmerited favor. If you are strong, mighty and wise in yourself, then God's unmerited favor cannot flow. But when you realize your weaknesses and foolishness, and depend on Jesus instead, *that* is when His unmerited favor can flow unhindered in your life.

When you acknowledge your weaknesses and depend on Jesus,
His unmerited favor can flow unhindered in your life.

We see this in the story of Moses. In his first 40 years as an Egyptian prince who was looked up to and admired, he thought that he knew everything. The Bible says that in this first 40 years, Moses was "mighty in words and deeds" (Acts 7:22), but God could not use him. However, in the next 40 years, something happened to Moses. He had fled Egypt after killing an Egyptian who was beating a Hebrew, and went to dwell in the Midian desert. He became a shepherd and was no longer considered mighty in words nor deeds. Indeed, he had even become a stutterer (Exodus 4:10). And at this point in his life, when he probably thought that he was a has-been, insignificant compared to what he had been, and that his glory-days were behind him, God appeared to him and said, "...I will send you to Pharaoh that you may bring My people...out of Egypt" (Exodus 3:10).

Forty years earlier, at the zenith of his ability, Moses could not even bury properly one Egyptian whom he had killed—he was found out and forced to flee (Exodus 2:11–15). But now, stripped of his dependence on his human strength and mindful of his weaknesses, he stepped into his call, dependent solely on the unmerited favor of God. And this time, when Moses waved his rod over the sea, the sea covered tens of thousands of Egyptians perfectly (Exodus 14:26–28).

The Bible tells us that "God resists the proud, but gives grace [unmerited favor] to the humble" (1 Peter 5:5). Beloved, God will not impose His unmerited favor on us. Whenever we want to depend on ourselves and our wisdom, He will allow us to do so. His unmerited favor is given to those who humbly acknowledge that they cannot succeed in their own strength and ability. When we let go and depend on His unmerited favor, He will take over and do for us what we cannot do for ourselves!

❖

Today's Prayer

Father, I humbly acknowledge my utter inability to accomplish anything in life in and of myself. Therefore, I turn away from my reliance on self-effort, and I choose to rely on You and Your unmerited favor alone. There can only be good results in my life when YOU are the one working in and through me. Any good success that I have today is because of You and Your unmerited favor. Thank You for doing for me and through me what I cannot do in and of myself.

Today's Thought
*When it is not me but God Himself working in
and through me, the results are perfect!*

Today's Reflection On Favor

_____

_____

_____

_____

_____

_____

_____

_____

_____

_____

_____

_____

_____

_____

_____

_____

_____

_____

_____

_____

_____

Submission Releases God's Favor Into Your Life

❖

Today's Scripture

Then Jesse said to his son David, "Take now for your brothers an ephah of this dried grain and these ten loaves, and run to your brothers at the camp. And carry these ten cheeses to the captain of their thousand..."
—1 Samuel 17:17–18

WHEN GOD WANTED to bring down a mighty giant who was terrorizing the nation of Israel, He sent someone who was weak in the flesh. Think about it. In the eyes of the world, what could be weaker against a trained and fearsome soldier than a young boy who had no formal military training, no armor, was dressed in a humble shepherd's garb, and did not even carry any real weapons other than a sling and five smooth stones from a brook? It is no wonder that Goliath mocked this young shepherd boy and his strategy. When David stepped into the battlefield, Goliath asked him sarcastically, "Am I a dog, that you come to me with sticks?" (1 Samuel 17:43).

Submission to God-appointed leadership will always cause God's favor to flow in your life.

The implications of this battle were massive. It was not just a duel or contest between two individuals. The Israelites and Philistines had agreed to each send a warrior who would represent their nation. The defeated warrior would commit his entire nation to become servants to the other nation. It would be an understatement to say that a whole lot was riding on this one fight. And who does God send to represent Israel? In natural terms, He sent possibly the most unqualified person onto that battlefield in the Valley of Elah.

David was not even a soldier in the army of Israel! Do you remember how this shepherd boy ended up at the battlefield to begin with? David was there to deliver bread and cheese to his brothers who were in the army (1 Samuel 17:17–20)! And yet, David found himself standing on the battlefield as Israel's representative against the haughty Goliath. From delivering bread and cheese, he was now called upon to deliver the entire nation of Israel.

David was at the right place at the right time because he humbled himself and submitted to his father's instructions to deliver bread and cheese to his brothers. Beloved, this is something you need to understand. Submission to God-appointed leadership will always cause God's favor to flow in your life, and you will find yourself, like David, at the right place at the right time!

The Bible says that we should not despise the day of humble beginnings (Zechariah 4:10). There is nothing glamorous about delivering bread and cheese, but David did not despise it. And that put him right in the Valley of Elah, the wind blowing in his hair—a young shepherd boy with no military experience representing the nation of Israel against a mighty giant who was a man of war from his youth.

This is what God loves to do. He loves to take the foolish and weak things to shame the wise and mighty things of the world. So beloved, humble yourself and submit to the authorities that God has placed above you. And when you are faithful to carry out small tasks assigned to you, His favor is released in your life and you might just find yourself doing great exploits for God!

❖

Today's Prayer

Father, I thank You that You can use the most unlikely people to do great exploits for You. You qualify the unqualified, exalt the lowly and turn underdogs into champions. Even small beginnings can have great endings when Your unmerited favor is released. Father, I choose to submit to the authorities You have placed over me in the different areas of my life and I will not despise any small task You have for me. Cause me to be at the right place at the right time, so that I can experience all the goodness that You have in store for me.

Today's Thought

Submission releases God's favor into my life.

Today's Reflection On Favor

_____

_____

_____

_____

_____

_____

_____

_____

_____

_____

_____

_____

_____

_____

_____

_____

DAY 94

How Esther Obtained Favor

❖

Today's Scripture

Now when the turn came for Esther the daughter of Abihail the uncle of Mordecai, who had taken her as his daughter, to go in to the king, she requested nothing but what Hegai the king's eunuch, the custodian of the women, advised. And Esther obtained favor in the sight of all who saw her. —Esther 2:15

WHEN YOU KNOW that you are greatly blessed, highly favored and deeply loved, you don't have to depend on your self-efforts. Look at the story of Esther, for example. When King Ahasuerus was looking for a new queen, the most beautiful women in the land were all brought into the palace. All the women were given the opportunity to adorn themselves with whatever they desired from the women's quarters before they were brought for an audience with the king. But when it was Esther's turn, she "requested nothing but what Hegai the king's eunuch, the custodian of the women, advised." And look at the results: "Esther **obtained favor** in the sight of all who saw her," and the king "loved Esther more than all the other women, and she **obtained grace and favor in his sight** more than all the virgins; so he set the royal crown upon her head and made her queen..." (Esther 2:17)

When the Lord promotes you, He gives you the influence to be a blessing to the people around you!

While the other women grabbed the best garments, perfumes and accessories to beautify themselves, Esther did not rely on her own abilities but submitted herself to Hegai, the official who had been appointed by the king to oversee the women. There was so much wisdom and humility in her decision. Can you see the beauty of Esther? She did not trust in her own efforts. While the women tried to outdo one another by relying on their own efforts, Esther wisely submitted to the one person who would know the king's preferences best, and the results speak for themselves.

This incident also demonstrates to us that Esther depended entirely upon the Lord's unmerited favor. (When you depend entirely upon the Lord's unmerited favor, you are trusting Him and in a position of rest.) Esther did not have to struggle. When she rested in the Lord and humbled herself, the Lord promoted her and exalted her above all the other beautiful women. God resists the proud and gives unmerited favor to the humble (1 Peter 5:5). When you humble yourself and cease from your efforts to promote yourself, and depend on Jesus alone, the Lord Himself will be your promotion and increase. Like Esther, you will stand out in a crowd and obtain grace and favor with God and man.

Do you know why the story of Esther is so important? Read the details in the Book of Esther. Because Esther was promoted to become the queen, she was in a favored position to protect all the Jewish people in the kingdom from being killed. When the Lord promotes you, He gives you the influence to be a blessing to the people around you. There are no coincidences, only God-incidents. The Lord will bless you to be a blessing!

❖

Today's Prayer

Father, I thank You that I don't have to rely on man to get promoted. I thank You that I don't have to scheme or struggle to get recognition from people. Jesus Himself is my promotion and increase. Lord Jesus, I depend on You, Your timing and Your unmerited favor. And when I do get promoted by Your unmerited favor, I thank You that it will be a position of influence, where I can be a blessing to others.

Today's Thought

The Lord Himself is my promotion and increase.

Today's Reflection On Favor

_____

_____

_____

_____

_____

_____

_____

_____

_____

_____

_____

_____

_____

_____

_____

_____

_____

_____

Personalize God's Favor In Your Life

❖

Today's Scripture

Then Peter, turning around, saw the disciple whom Jesus loved following, who also had leaned on His breast at the supper, and said, "Lord, who is the one who betrays You?" —John 21:20

I USED TO think that among Jesus' 12 disciples, John was the Lord's favorite disciple and the one who was the closest to Him because the Bible calls John "the disciple whom Jesus loved." I was under the impression that John had a special favor with Jesus, and always wondered what made him so special that he stood apart from the other disciples. Don't you want to be known as the disciple whom Jesus loves? I do!

It is your prerogative to see yourself as the disciple whom Jesus loves, and to call yourself that!

Then one day, when I was reading God's Word, the secret of John's favor dawned on me. The Lord opened my eyes and showed me that the phrase "the disciple whom Jesus loved" is actually found only in John's own book! Check it out for yourself. You will not find this phrase being used in the Gospels of Matthew, Mark and Luke. It is found only in the Gospel of John. It is a phrase that John used to describe himself!

Now, what was John doing? He was **practicing and personalizing the love that Jesus had for him**. We are all God's favorites, but John knew the secret of accessing Jesus' unmerited favor for himself. It is your prerogative to see yourself as the disciple whom Jesus loves, and to call yourself that!

When I started to teach that the secret of John's favor lay in his personalization of God's love, the people in my church literally stepped into a new dimension of experiencing God's unmerited favor in their lives. I have seen how some of them really took this revelation and ran with it. Some of them customized the wallpapers of their cell phones to say "The disciple whom Jesus loves," while others signed off their text messages and emails with the phrase.

As they kept reminding themselves that they are the disciple whom Jesus loves, they began to grow in the consciousness of the Lord's love for them. At the same time, they began to grow in being favor-conscious! I have piles of praise reports on how our congregation members have been so blessed just by being conscious of Jesus' favor in their lives. Some of them have been promoted, some have received spectacular increments to their paychecks and many have won various prizes at company functions and in other contests, including all-expense-paid vacations.

A brother from my church signed up for a certain credit card during a special promotion in which new applicants stood to win a range of prizes. There were probably hundreds of thousands of people who participated in this promotion, but this young man just believed that *he* was highly favored, and because of that, *he* would win the top prize.

The day of the draw came and true enough, this young man won the top prize—a stunning black Lamborghini Gallardo! When he wrote to the church to share his testimony, he enclosed a picture of himself smiling from ear to ear, posing with his brand-new Lamborghini. He said that he knew that he had won the car by the unmerited favor of God, and after he had sold off the car, he brought his tithe to the church, giving all glory and honor to Jesus. The world calls this "luck," but for the believer, there is no such thing as luck. There is only the unmerited favor of Jesus!

❖

Today's Prayer

Father, in so loving the world, You so love me. Thank You for lavishing Your unconditional and personal love on me. I see myself embraced by You, and watched over by You. I am the apple of Your eye—the disciple whom You love! And because Your love for me is fathomless and personal, I expect good things to happen to me today. I thank You for favor with people. I thank You for divine protection. I thank You for abundant provision and right happenings today!

Today's Thought

I am the disciple whom Jesus loves!

Today's Reflection On Favor

_____

_____

_____

_____

_____

_____

_____

_____

_____

_____

_____

_____

_____

_____

_____

_____

_____

_____

Always Remember That You Are God's Beloved

❖

Today's Scripture

Having predestined us to adoption as sons by Jesus Christ to Himself, according to the good pleasure of His will, to the praise of the glory of His grace, by which He made us accepted in the Beloved. —*Ephesians 1:5–6*

Do you believe that you are beloved and highly favored by God? Ephesians 1:6 says, "to the praise of the glory of His grace [unmerited favor], by which He made us accepted in the Beloved." It is not possible for us to make ourselves accepted. We are made accepted by the glory of the Lord's unmerited favor. The word "accepted" in Ephesians 1:6 is the Greek word *charitoo*. Now, the root word for *charitoo* is *charis*,[1] which means "grace." So *charitoo* simply means "highly graced" or "highly favored." In other words, you are highly favored in the Beloved!

For the devil's temptations to work, he cannot remind you that you are God's beloved.

Now, we know that "the Beloved" in Ephesians 1:6 refers to Jesus. If you read on, it says in the next verse that "In Him [Jesus the Beloved] we have redemption through His blood, the forgiveness of sins, according to the riches of His grace [unmerited favor]." Now, why didn't the Bible just say that we are highly favored in Jesus or in Christ? (There are no insignificant details in the Bible.) Why did the Holy Spirit choose specifically to say that we are highly favored **"in the Beloved"**?

"Beloved" is a warm and intimate term that was used by God at the Jordan River to describe Jesus. The Bible tells us that when Jesus was baptized in the Jordan River, as soon as He came up from the water, "He saw the heavens parting and the Spirit descending upon Him like a dove. Then a voice came from heaven, 'You are My **beloved Son**, in whom I am **well pleased**'" (Mark 1:10–11). In these scriptures, you can see the triune God—God the Father, the Son and the Holy Spirit. This tells us that there is something very important for us to learn here.

God the Father spoke publicly and His words were recorded for you to know that to be "accepted in the Beloved" means that God is **well pleased** with **you** today. See yourself sandwiched right smack in the midst of Jesus, God's Beloved. When God looks at you, He doesn't see you in your failures and shortcomings. He sees you in Jesus' perfection and loveliness! Because you are in Christ, God says to **you**, "You, _____ (insert your name here), are My beloved, in whom I am well pleased." Jesus is well-pleasing to God because He kept the law perfectly. You and I are well-pleasing to God because we are accepted and highly favored in the Beloved, who took all our sins and fulfilled the law on our behalf!

Immediately after Jesus was baptized, He was led into the wilderness to be tempted by the devil. The devil came to Jesus and said, "If You are the Son of God, command that these stones become bread" (Matthew 4:3). Now, don't forget that Jesus had just heard the voice of His Father affirming Him with the words "You are My beloved Son." Years ago, as I was studying Jesus' temptations by the devil, the Lord asked me, "Did you notice that the devil dropped one word when he came to tempt My Son?"

I had never heard anyone preach this before or read this in any book, but God opened my eyes to see that the devil had omitted the word "beloved"! God had just told Jesus, "You are My **beloved** Son." But shortly after that, the devil came to Jesus, saying, "If You are the Son of God..." The word "beloved" is missing! The serpent had deliberately left out the word "beloved"!

The Lord then showed me that for the devil's temptations to work,

275

he cannot remind you that you are God's beloved. The moment you are reminded of your identity as God's beloved in Christ, he will not be able to succeed! It is no wonder that the devil wants to rob believers of their sense of being God's beloved. So don't fall for the devil's trick. Remind yourself today and every day that you **are** God's beloved!

Today's Prayer

Father, I thank You that You accept, love and favor me because I am found in Christ, Your Beloved. I did not do anything to deserve this— it is all Christ and Your undeserved favor. Help me to always be conscious of the fact that I am Your beloved child. Thank You for showing me that the more conscious I am of this truth, the more the devil's temptations cannot succeed in my life. Today, I expect good things to happen to me—just because I am Your beloved child!

Today's Thought

I am God's beloved and highly favored in Christ the Beloved.

Today's Reflection On Favor

_____

_____

_____

_____

_____

_____

_____

_____

_____

_____

Feed On God's Love Daily

❖

Today's Scripture

For God so loved the world that He gave His only begotten Son, that whoever believes in Him should not perish but have everlasting life.
—John 3:16

M<small>Y FRIEND,</small> G<small>OD</small> wants you to live each day knowing that you are His beloved child, in whom He is well pleased. That is your daily nourishment from Him—to know, believe and confess that you are His beloved and that you are well-pleasing to Him all the time.

Live each day feeding on God's love, grace, perfect acceptance of and unmerited favor toward you.

So live each day feeding on God's love, grace, perfect acceptance of and unmerited favor toward you. When you do so, you are reminding yourself that you are His beloved no matter what happens to you. When you are constantly full of the consciousness of His favor on your life, nothing can get you down. You will have such a confidence of God's goodness toward you that even when the devil starts throwing lemons at you, you know that God will turn those lemons into refreshing lemonade for you! You begin to have a confident expectation of good even when circumstances in the natural don't look so great. That is walking by faith in Jesus' goodness, and not by sight. You are no longer looking at your challenges. You are looking at Jesus' face shining upon you and imparting grace into your situation.

When you are confident that you are God's beloved, not only will you overcome the devil's temptations, you will dare to ask Him to bless you even in the little things. Many years ago, Wendy and I went to a restaurant for dinner when she was pregnant with Jessica. As we were about to order our food, a man seated not too far away from us took out a pack of cigarettes and prepared to take a smoke. I really didn't want Wendy to take in any of that secondhand cigarette smoke, but there was no nonsmoking section in that restaurant. So guess what I did? I prayed! Under my breath, I told the Lord, "Lord, I know that I am Your beloved. Please stop that man from smoking in this restaurant." That was all I said—a quick and simple prayer.

Guess what happened? That man tried to light his cigarette, but he just could not get his lighter to work! He persisted and kept trying, but no matter what he did, the lighter simply would not work. After some time, he shoved his cigarettes back in his shirt pocket in frustration. Praise Jesus! Even in the little things, God hears and answers the prayers of His beloved. Nothing is too big or too small for your Daddy God. If it matters to you, it matters to Him. When you know that you are His beloved, you can walk in constant expectation of His unmerited favor in every situation!

Some years ago, I was taking a cab in New York and I took the opportunity to share the love of Jesus with the driver. Her response was quite typical. She said flippantly, "God loves everybody, man!"

It is absolutely true that God loves everybody, but to experience His love firsthand in your life, you have to **personalize His love for you**. Jesus died for you and do you know that even if you were the only person on earth, God would still have sent His Son to die on the cross for you? That is how precious YOU are to Him!

You need to personalize John 3:16 by declaring, "For God so loved _____ (insert your name), He sent His only begotten Son to die on the cross for _____ (insert your name)." Be like the disciple John, who personalized the Lord's love for him by calling himself "the disciple whom Jesus loved."

The sun shines on every blade of grass in a field. But if you put a magnifying glass over one particular blade of grass, it will center the heat from the sun over that blade, and that blade of grass will burn. That is what you must do with God's love. Put a magnifying glass over your life and imagine God's love being focused and concentrated on YOU! When you personalize God's love for YOU, when you live each day knowing that God loves YOU, **you** will be blazing with a supernatural ability to overcome every challenge in life!

❖

Today's Prayer

Father, I thank You that I am Your beloved child, precious in Your sight. Because You are God, You can so love the whole world and still love me with a personal love. Your goodness toward me enables me to soar above the storms of life. Even when the devil throws lemons at me, You will turn those lemons into refreshing lemonade for me! Today, I see You smiling on me as I stand under the spotlight of Your unconditional love and unmerited favor. I call this day blessed and full of right happenings for me!

Today's Thought

I can ask God for big or small things. If it matters to me, it matters to Him because I am His beloved!

Today's Reflection On Favor

_____

_____

_____

_____

_____

_____

_____

DAY 98

Rest In Jesus' Finished Work

Today's Scripture

But God, who is rich in mercy, because of His great love with which He loved us, even when we were dead in trespasses, made us alive together with Christ (by grace you have been saved), and raised us up together, and made us sit together in the heavenly places in Christ Jesus, that in the ages to come He might show the exceeding riches of His grace [unmerited favor] in His kindness toward us in Christ Jesus.
—Ephesians 2:4–7

LOOK AT THE above passage. It tells us that by God's unmerited favor, we are seated together with Christ at the Father's right hand. What does it mean to be seated together in the heavenly places in Christ Jesus? It means that today, we are in a position of rest in Jesus' finished work. To be *seated* in Christ is to *rest*, to trust in Him, and to receive everything our beautiful Savior has accomplished on our behalf. My friend, God wants us to take the position of relying on Jesus for good success in every area of our lives, instead of relying on our good works and human efforts to achieve success. What a blessing it is to be in this position of dependence on our Savior!

To be seated in Christ is to rest, to trust in Him, and to receive everything our beautiful Savior has accomplished on our behalf.

But instead of looking at Jesus, believers are misled by the devil into **looking at themselves**. For thousands of years, the devil's strategy has not changed. He is a master at accusing you, pointing out all your flaws, weaknesses, mistakes and blemishes. He will keep on reminding you of your past failures and use condemnation to perpetuate the cycle of defeat in your life.

When the apostle Paul found himself sinking into self-occupation, he became depressed and cried out, "O wretched man that I am! Who will deliver me...?" (Romans 7:24). In the very next verse, he sees God's solution and says, "I thank God—through Jesus Christ our Lord!" Likewise, beloved, it's time for you to step out from being self-conscious and self-occupied, and begin to be Christ-occupied instead.

Today, you should no longer be asking yourself, "Am I accepted before God?" This question puts the focus back on you and this places you under the law. I know that there are people who will encourage you to ask yourself this question, but it is an error to ask yourself if you are accepted before God. The correct question to ask is, "Is Christ accepted before God?" because as Christ is, so are you in this world (1 John 4:17). Don't ask, "Am I pleasing to God?" Instead, ask, "Is Christ pleasing to God?" Can you see the difference in emphasis? The old covenant of law is all about **you**, but the new covenant of grace is all about **Jesus**! The law places the demand on you to perform and makes you self-conscious, whereas grace places the demand on Jesus and makes you Jesus-conscious.

Can you imagine a young child growing up and always wondering in his heart, "Am I pleasing to Daddy? Am I pleasing to Mummy? Do Daddy and Mummy accept me?" This child will grow up emotionally warped if he does not have the security and assurance of his parents' love and acceptance. That is why your loving heavenly Father wants you rooted, established and anchored in His unwavering love for you. He demonstrated His love for you when He sent Jesus to become your sin on the cross so that you can become His righteousness. Our part today is to turn away from ourselves and to look at Jesus!

❖

Today's Prayer

Father, it gladdens my heart to know that You see me in Christ and not in my flesh. Despite all my faults, as Christ is accepted before You today, so am I accepted and loved by You today. As Christ is pleasing to You, so am I pleasing to You. As He is before You, so am I in this world because You have placed me in Him. I rest in Christ and all that He has accomplished for me. Father, help me keep my eyes on Jesus, my victory and my true and unchanging identity.

Today's Thought

Resting in Christ is relying on Jesus, instead of my self-efforts, for good success in every area of my life.

Today's Reflection On Favor

_____

_____

_____

_____

_____

_____

_____

_____

_____

_____

_____

_____

_____

_____

DAY 99

Meditate On God's Word

❖

Today's Scripture

This Book of the Law shall not depart from your mouth, but you shall meditate in it day and night, that you may observe to do according to all that is written in it. For then you will make your way prosperous, and then you will have good success. —Joshua 1:8

Look at the instructions that God gave Joshua when he was appointed as Moses' successor: "This Book of the Law shall not depart from your mouth, but you shall meditate in it day and night, that you may observe to do according to all that is written in it. For then you will make your way **prosperous**, and then you will have **good success**." God told Joshua that to have good success, he had to meditate on the law day and night. Joshua lived under the old covenant, so how should we, who live under the new covenant, benefit from this scripture?

The secret to good success is found in meditating on God's Word in the light of the new covenant of grace.

We need to read this portion of scripture in view of Jesus' finished work. That is why it is essential for you to be firmly established on the rock-solid foundation of the new covenant of grace. Now that you know that we are no longer under the law, what is the new covenant way to be blessed and to experience good success? Joshua only had the law to meditate upon because the New Testament had not been written yet. For us, the secret to good success is found in meditating on God's Word in the light of the **new covenant of grace**.

Before we can go into what it means to meditate on God's Word, what exactly does it mean to "meditate"?

When the Bible talks about meditation, it's not referring to a mental exercise. The Hebrew word for meditation in the Old Testament is the word *hagah*, which means to utter or mutter.[1] So to *hagah* is to speak under your breath. Notice that the Lord told Joshua, "This Book of the Law shall not depart from your **mouth**..." He did not say that it "shall not depart from your mind." The key to meditating on God's Word is not mental contemplation. It is in speaking God's promises with your mouth!

"Pastor Prince, does this mean that I should keep repeating God's Word? For instance, should I keep saying 'by His stripes I am healed' when I need healing?"

Meditating on God's Word does not mean making vain repetitions of scriptures. It is much more and is something that first occurs deep in your heart. The psalmist David captured the essence of meditation most aptly when he said, "My heart was hot within me; while I was musing, the fire burned. Then I spoke with my tongue" (Psalm 39:3). As you are meditating on God's Word, ask the Holy Spirit to give you a fresh revelation of Jesus. Let that scripture burn with revelation in your heart. And as you speak out of that burning revelation, God anoints the words that you speak. When you declare, "By His stripes I am healed," and that declaration is uttered with a sense of revelation and faith in Jesus, there will be power in your declaration!

❖

Today's Prayer

Father, I thank You that Your will is to prosper me and give me good success that will not destroy me. Give me a heart that desires to meditate on Your Word and I ask that You speak to me words of life whenever I meditate on Your Word. Give me fresh revelations of Your Son Jesus—the loveliness of His person and the perfection of His finished work.

Today's Thought
Meditation brings revelation that delivers
power to my declarations.

Today's Reflection On Favor

_____

_____

_____

_____

_____

_____

_____

_____

_____

_____

_____

_____

_____

_____

_____

_____

_____

_____

_____

_____

DAY 100

Right Living Is A Result Of Right Believing

❖

Today's Scripture

For as he thinks in his heart, so is he... —*Proverbs 23:7*

In preaching grace over the years, some people have asked me this: "Don't you think that our performance is important?" I tell them that our performance is important, absolutely. But I also tell them that our performance as husbands, wives, parents, students, employees and children of God is a **result** of believing that we are righteous by faith. I say this over and over again, and I will never grow tired of saying it: Right living is a result of right believing. There are a lot of people preaching and focusing on right living. For them, right living is always about becoming more holy, fearing God more, doing more, praying more, reading the Bible more, serving in church more or giving more money to help the needy. But my friend, when you focus on external behavior alone, you are only dealing with superficial elements.

Believe right and you will live right. The opposite is also true: Believe wrong and you will live wrong.

While strong preaching on holiness may have a temporal effect on people's behavior, it will not bring about lasting and permanent change. Let me give you an analogy. If you cut off the weeds in your garden but fail to remove their roots, in no time at all, the weeds will grow again in your garden. That is what preaching about right living does in the church. Temporarily, the problem may appear to be resolved, but as long as the roots are still alive, the same wrong behavior, the same evil habits and the same addictions will appear again, just like stubborn weeds.

For decades, the church has preached about right living, with no results of long-lasting or permanent change in people's behavior. It is time for us to go after the root, and the root is not in preaching right living, but in preaching **right believing**. Believe right and you will live right. The opposite is also true: Believe wrong and you will live wrong. Christianity is not about behavior modification. It is about inward heart transformation. Start addressing the root instead and get hold of good teachings that are full of Jesus and righteousness by faith in Him. When you are anchored on these unshakable foundations, your outward behavior will come in line with His Word and you will begin to be transformed into His image from glory to glory! You will produce the fruits of righteousness!

Just in case there is any misunderstanding, let me state this clearly in black and white: I, Joseph Prince, **hate sin** and wrong living. As a pastor of a local church for more than two decades now, I have witnessed firsthand the devastating effects of sin. It destroys marriages, breaks up families, brings diseases and basically tears a person apart from the inside out. I am on the same side as those who preach against sin and teach on the need to live right. However, where I differ is that I believe that the solution to stopping sin is not found in focusing on right living. It is found in **right believing**.

I believe the best of God's children. I believe that true born-again believers in Jesus are not looking for opportunities to sin, but are looking for the power to overcome and reign over sin. Even if their actions may not be altogether there yet, I believe that they already know that they *should* live right, and desire to do so. So I believe my part as a pastor is to help them believe right first. When they believe right, and know that they are righteous by faith and not by their works, they *will* live right.

We see in the Bible that the traits of right living include self-control, perseverance, brotherly kindness and love (2 Peter 1:5–7). But did you know that the Bible also tells us why some believers lack these qualities? It says in 2 Peter 1:9, "For he who lacks these things is shortsighted, even to blindness, and has forgotten that he was cleansed from his old sins." Wow! This verse is essentially telling us that the reason someone does not manifest these qualities of right living is that he has forgotten that all his sins have been forgiven and that he is righteous by faith in Jesus. It isn't something he believes and is conscious of, and it affects his behavior.

So start believing right, and you will live right! If you don't see right living in a particular area of your life—perhaps you are struggling with a secret addiction—check what you believe in that area. Somewhere along the way, you have believed a lie. But here's the good news: When you start seeing and believing that you are righteous in Christ, when you start confessing your righteousness through Jesus in that area, your breakthrough is just around the corner. Beloved, remember and believe this every day: Jesus wants to free you, prosper you and give you good success!

❖

Today's Prayer

Father, thank You for reminding me that all my sins have been forgiven and that I am righteous by faith in Jesus Christ. Thank You for also showing me that right believing leads to right living. For the areas of my life where I am not living right, I ask that You show me where I have believed wrong, so that I may renew my mind with Your Word and believe right. I choose to believe that You want to set me free, prosper me and give me good success!

Believe right first, then I will live right and
see blessings and breakthroughs.

Today's Reflection On Favor

_____

_____

_____

_____

_____

_____

_____

_____

_____

_____

_____

_____

_____

_____

_____

_____

_____

_____

_____

_____

_____

Salvation Prayer

If you would like to receive all that Jesus has done for you, and make Him your Lord and Savior, please pray this prayer:

Lord Jesus, thank You for loving me and dying for me on the cross. Your precious blood washes me clean of every sin. You are my Lord and my Savior, now and forever. I believe that You rose from the dead and that You are alive today. Because of Your finished work, I am now a beloved child of God and heaven is my home. Thank You for giving me eternal life, and filling my heart with Your peace and joy. Amen.

We Would Like To Hear From You

If you have prayed the salvation prayer or if you have a testimony to share after reading this book, please tell us about it via JosephPrince.com/testimony.

Stay Connected With Joseph

Connect with Joseph through these social media channels and receive daily inspirational teachings:

Facebook.com/JosephPrince
Twitter.com/JosephPrince
Youtube.com/JosephPrinceOnline
Instagram: @JosephPrince

Notes

Day 2

1. NT:5547, Biblesoft's New Exhaustive Strong's Numbers and Concordance with Expanded Greek-Hebrew Dictionary. Copyright © 1994, 2003, 2006 Biblesoft, Inc. and International Bible Translators, Inc.

Day 23

1. NT:3364, Biblesoft's New Exhaustive Strong's Numbers and Concordance with Expanded Greek-Hebrew Dictionary. Copyright © 1994, 2003, 2006 Biblesoft, Inc. and International Bible Translators, Inc.

Day 43

1. Carl Stuart Hamblen, "Is He Satisfied With Me?" I Believe, Hamblen Music Company, 1952.

Day 46

1. NT:2842, Biblesoft's New Exhaustive Strong's Numbers and Concordance with Expanded Greek-Hebrew Dictionary. Copyright © 1994, 2003, 2006 Biblesoft, Inc. and International Bible Translators, Inc.

Day 48

1. Coverdale's Dedication and Preface, Coverdale's Bible. Retrieved 23 April 2009 from www.bible-researcher.com/coverdale1.html

Day 53

1. OT:7965, The Online Bible Thayer's Greek Lexicon and Brown Driver & Briggs Hebrew Lexicon, Copyright © 1993, Woodside Bible Fellowship, Ontario, Canada. Licensed from the Institute for Creation Research.

Day 66

1. NT:2889, Thayer's Greek Lexicon, Electronic Database. Copyright © 2000, 2003, 2006 by Biblesoft, Inc. All rights reserved.

Day 69

1. Hitchcock's Bible Names Dictionary, PC Study Bible formatted electronic database Copyright © 2003, 2006 Biblesoft, Inc. All rights reserved.

Day 75

1. OT:7136, The Online Bible Thayer's Greek Lexicon and Brown Driver & Briggs Hebrew Lexicon, Copyright © 1993, Woodside Bible Fellowship, Ontario, Canada. Licensed from the Institute for Creation Research.

Notes

Day 76

1. OT:4745, Biblesoft's New Exhaustive Strong's Numbers and Concordance with Expanded Greek-Hebrew Dictionary. Copyright © 1994, 2003, 2006 Biblesoft, Inc. and International Bible Translators, Inc.

2. The unnamed servant is probably Eliezer of Damascus, Abraham's chief servant.

Day 82

1. OT:8085, Biblesoft's New Exhaustive Strong's Numbers and Concordance with Expanded Greek-Hebrew Dictionary. Copyright © 1994, 2003, 2006 Biblesoft, Inc. and International Bible Translators, Inc.

Day 85

1. Prince, Joseph. (2007). Destined To Reign. Singapore: 22 Media Pte Ltd. p.208–209.

Day 90

1. NT:5487, Biblesoft's New Exhaustive Strong's Numbers and Concordance with Expanded Greek-Hebrew Dictionary. Copyright © 1994, 2003, 2006 Biblesoft, Inc. and International Bible Translators, Inc.

Day 96

1. NT:5485, Biblesoft's New Exhaustive Strong's Numbers and Concordance with Expanded Greek-Hebrew Dictionary. Copyright © 1994, 2003, 2006 Biblesoft, Inc. and International Bible Translators, Inc.

Day 99

1. OT:1897, The Online Bible Thayer's Greek Lexicon and Brown Driver & Briggs Hebrew Lexicon, Copyright © 1993, Woodside Bible Fellowship, Ontario, Canada. Licensed from the Institute for Creation Research.